THE
ORGANIC
HERB
GARDENER

THE ORGANIC HERB GARDENER

Graham Clarke

GUILD OF MASTER
CRAFTSMAN PUBLICATIONS

First published 2010 by
Guild of Master Craftsman Publications Ltd
Castle Place, 166 High Street, Lewes,
East Sussex BN7 1XU

ISBN 978-1-86108-683-9

Associate Publisher: Jonathan Bailey
Production Manager: Jim Bulley
Managing Editor: Gerrie Purcell
Senior Project Editor: Virginia Brehaut
Copy Editor: Judith Chamberlain-Webber
Managing Art Editor: Gilda Pacitti
Design: Chloë Alexander

Set in Nofret and Helvetica Neue
Colour origination by GMC Reprographics
Printed and bound in China by Hing Yip Printing Co. Ltd

Contents

1 Herbs and the organic gardener

2 Planning a herb garden

3 Propagating herbs

4 Buying and planting herbs

5 Caring for herbs

6 Organic pest and disease control

7 Harvesting, drying and preserving herbs

8 Calendar of work

9 Directory of herbs

Introduction

GROWING HERBS is a real joy. They can look fantastic in a garden, as they often have silvery or variegated foliage in tight, compact mounds. Many types have bright flowers, too. They can be highly fragrant, which makes them ideal plants for sensory gardens and gardens for children. Herbs do, of course, have a value other than pure decoration, and for many gardeners the main reason for growing them is so they can be used in the kitchen for flavouring food, or elsewhere for medicinal, cosmetic or for other household use.

But what does the word 'herb' actually mean? It is really just a shortened form of the word 'herbaceous', which is defined as a type of plant that lacks a woody stem, and dies down to the ground at the end of its growing season, or life if the plant is an annual. However, this definition does not apply to some of the more familiar of our traditional herbs, such as lavender, sage and thyme. These, and many others like them, are woody and do not die down. So, although we can see how the word 'herb' originated, it is now used to mean something else.

The old herbals

The word 'herb' has given birth to other words and terms that are quite specific, and these include 'herbal' and 'herbalism'. Both are long-standing words that are used exclusively in the context of growing or using plants for the betterment of one's health and/ or lifestyle. The first time the word 'herbal' found its way into common vocabulary was in the 1597 book by 'herbalist' John Gerard. Entitled *Great Herball*, or *General Histoire of Plantes*, it is better known to 21st-century commentators as simply 'Gerard's Herbal'. The author, it is said, grew more than 1,000 species of herbs in his garden.

Some 30 years after this, botanist John Parkinson catalogued more than 3,000 species of herbs. Shortly after that Nicholas Culpeper brought out *The Complete Herbal*, which included medicinal and astrological information (which many at the time believed was significant in the growing of such plants).

Herbs and the Ancient World

HERBS HAVE been used for thousands of years. Babylonian clay tablets some 5,000 years old depict medical treatments using herbs, and within the following millennium cultures in China, Assyria, Egypt and India all issued written records of herb use in medicine.

The Chinese, particularly, were the pioneers of herb use. For example, to the Chinese the *Chrysanthemum* is both useful and beautiful, but it is also virtuous. This plant has been widely grown for its medicinal properties, and valued for having positive effects on the liver, joints, eyes, headache and appetite.

Egyptian writings from 1,550 BC contain medical prescriptions and notes on the aromatic and cosmetic uses of herbs, especially in relation to their use in religious ceremonies. Some 2,000 years later, around AD 500, the Greek and Roman interest in herbs culminated in the publication of *De Materia Medica* by the Greek physician, botanist and pharmacologist Pedanius Dioscorides. In it he described 600 healing plants, and it is the earliest surviving herbal with illustrations.

▶ **A variety of herbs, even in a small garden, can be both functional and decorative.**

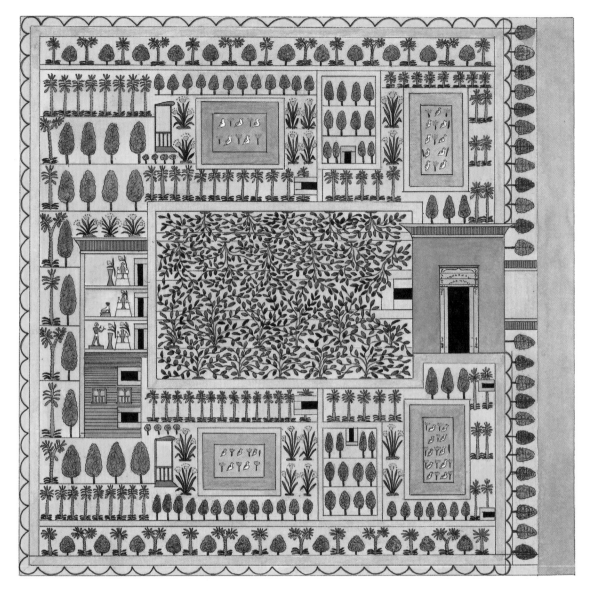

▲ **This Ancient Egyptian garden shows very precise planting. Many plants were grown for medicinal use.**

Although herbs started as subjects of medicine, it was the Romans who first used them widely in cooking. Fascinating and adventurous herbal combinations were tried, such as globe artichokes cooked in a mixture of fennel, mint, rue and coriander, pounded together and then added to pepper, lovage, honey, oil and liquamen (a strong fish sauce regularly used as a substitute for salt).

By the Tudor times in Britain, herbs had become a staple of daily life. In 1699 the botanist John Evelyn wrote *Acetaria: A Discourse of Sallets.* In it he listed 73 salad herbs, giving details of the part of each herb used (root, stalk, leaf, flower, bud or seed) and how it was prepared (raw, chopped, steamed, blanched or pickled).

Publications about herbs became increasingly popular in the sixteenth and seventeenth centuries – which is where Gerard and Culpeper come in. Up to this time the herbals had been about the plants and their combined botanical and medicinal virtues: these two disciplines

▲ **Thyme is one of the most frequently grown herbs, for it has culinary, medicinal, cosmetic and household uses.**

were regarded almost as a single subject, in the apothecary style. But now science was beginning to emerge. Plants were being studied in minute detail and then classified. Botany and medicine went their separate ways. And as the science took over, with the possibility of manufacturing and synthesizing drugs, herbalism went into decline.

In 1931 an Englishwoman, Mrs M. Grieve (Sophia Emma Magdalene Grieve, also known as Margaret, Maude and Maud, but usually referred to simply as Mrs Grieve), wrote *A Modern Herbal*, which drew together scientific and traditional information. This happened at an opportune

Did you know?

Interestingly, even 200 years ago the word vegetable was not commonly used. Gardeners and cooks of the time referred to pot herbs (for bulk cooking in pots), salet herbs (for salad vegetables), sweet herbs (for flavourings) and simples (medicinal herbs from which compounds and poultices were made).

time, for there was renewed interest in the offerings of herbs, partly generated by the food and medical shortages following World War I. It seemed that even in the trenches, garlic, thyme and moss were used to play life–saving roles.

Over the centuries herbs have played a significant role in the development of Man. It is not an underestimation to say that herbs have changed the world.

Take, for example, the plant *Papaver somniferum*. A decorative plant in gardens today, 6,000 years ago it was being grown and used by Sumerians as a painkiller. In fact, there has never been a naturally occurring painkiller like it, and even today its derivatives are still the drugs of choice for relieving severe pain. It is also one of the most addictive substances known to Man. I am talking about opium, as a drug, and painkillers such as morphine, codeine and methadone, which have emanated from it. There was even major conflict (the Opium Wars of the 1840s) between Great Britain and China, when the latter country

banned the import of opium in an effort to tackle the domestic and social problems of addiction. Britain was the victor – and gained Hong Kong in the process.

Then there is the herb coca (*Erythroxylum coca*). When chewed, its leaves were used as a comforting and healing substance by the early peoples of Peru 1,500 years ago. In the 1850s its alkaloid – cocaine – was isolated, and used as a local anaesthetic for minor operations. Shortly after this, cocaine was popularized and used socially by the intelligentsia of the day, long before it became the scourge of society. Coca wine became a craze and, in 1886, a non–alcoholic version was launched by a US chemist, John Pemberton. He called it Coca–Cola®. The sale of cocaine was banned in 1902, so the formula of the soft drink changed and today's colas use only de–cocainized coca extracts.

We must not forget the herb meadowsweet (*Filipendula ulmaria*), which contains salicin. When synthesized it made an acceptable external

Poppy seed heads are decorative in their own right, whilst the seeds within them are a source of pain relief (in the form of painkillers) for millions.

Herbs can easily be slotted into any garden style, from large and formal to tiny cottage gardens and patio containers.

▲ **Herbs can be tall and wide or short and narrow, and with careful planning they can look very dramatic.**

skin treatment. Further refinement resulted in acetylsalicylic acid. It was given a simpler name, after *Spiraea ulmaria* (the old name for the plant), and that name was aspirin.

In the 21st century, herbs are as important as they ever were. Scientists are constantly searching and researching how herbs – plants in general – can be used, many in ground–breaking ideas for medicinal, cosmetic and decorative applications. As I write this book the television viewing week is heavily laden with cookery programmes in the scheduling, and a surge in

the culinary arts has prompted new interest in buying, growing and using fresh herbs. Combine this with an interest in foreign cuisine, where herbs from different parts of the world are used, plus the consistent call for improved nutrition, and you can see how and why herbs are important to us all.

This book is as much for the organic gardener as it is for the person keen to know more about choosing and growing herbs. As you will see in chapter one, herbs and organic principles are completely in harmony with each other.

So, how can this book help you to become a better organic gardener, with a supreme collection of good–quality, aromatic, tasty and

Did you know?

The decorative perennial plant known as lady's mantle (*Alchemilla mollis*), has been widely used medicinally to cure or ease internal symptoms in menstrual and menopausal women. It is easy therefore to see how the common name came about. The Latin name is relevant, too. Literally, it refers to the plant being used commonly (*mollis*) in alchemy (chemistry – and in particular pharmaceutical chemistry, as practised in the Middle Ages).

advice on herb selecting, buying, planting and aftercare is provided in the first half, along with key organic pointers, from companion planting and non–chemical control of pests, diseases and weeds, to organic soil–conditioning and fertilizer regimes. Herb choice is covered in depth in the directory starting on page 103.

As someone who was trained in conventional chemical–using horticulture, I saw the light 20 years ago when my first daughter was born, and have gardened organically ever since. But as far as herbs are concerned, I have grown them since the age of ten when my father gave me a plot in the family garden to call my own. It started with mint, and in succeeding gardens over the years the herb collection has now graduated to include more than 70 different types.

I hope, after reading this book, you will also be inspired to try as many different types as you can, and to grow them organically. It's completely rewarding – and utterly satisfying!

health–giving herbs? I have laboured long and hard into the night to identify all of the aspects of organic cultivation – as relating to herbs – and I am confident that all you need to know is included within the covers of this book. General

▼ **What distinguishes a herb from any other plant is that it can be cut and used indoors, often with many purposes.**

There are interesting synergies between the cultivation of herbs and the principles of organic gardening. At the risk of making sweeping generalizations, in my experience, if you are interested in growing herbs you will probably also be interested in a more organic and environmentally aware lifestyle.

Herbs and the organic gardener

Why herbs are ideal for the organic gardener

Growing herbs for culinary, medicinal, cosmetic and/or household purposes means you can avoid the mass-produced flavourings and chemicals that are found in most supermarket medicines, make-ups and household cleaners. You may be a reluctant user of such mass-produced products, or you

▲ **Herbs can be grown in so many situations. Here, sage is growing with climbing French beans.**

may be an avoider of them; either way, this attitude has the makings of a greener and more environmentally aware lifestyle.

If you grow herbs entirely for using in the kitchen, to flavour and enhance your food, then you almost certainly will be someone who can identify the often subtle differences in taste, texture, colour and so on. Yes, you can buy all the fresh herbs and spices you need from the supermarket, but as a gardener you also enjoy the growing aspect. So, as a discerning person who enjoys growing plants it is likely you will care about the environment. You will not want to be party to its ongoing destruction purely to satisfy your own taste buds!

◄ **Those people who grow herbs for use in the kitchen, or home in general, are likely to be organically inclined.**

From these five commonsense and fairly obvious indicators we can see that herb growers are more likely than most to be organically minded when it comes to their gardening and overall lifestyle. Or, looking at all of this another way, if one is perfectly content to buy all one's food flavourings, medicines, cosmetics and household products from the supermarket, with little regard to what is contained in them and how many food or product miles it has taken to get them to the shop's shelves, then one is probably not going to be a grower of herbs!

Once you understand how a sustainable lifestyle is conducive to the growing of herbs, you then have to examine what the herbs give back. Do they offer the organic gardener something in return? The answer is a resounding yes. In fact, I would go as far as to say that herbs are the perfect choice for any gardener who is organically inclined, and over the next few pages we will be looking at the reasons why.

Third, if you grow herbs mainly for medicinal and therapeutic purposes, you may be interested in alternative medicines and homeopathy. In my experience, such enthusiasts are not just aware of themselves and their own bodies, but are also aware of the importance of nature (and naturalistic remedies) as well as the wider world around them, and its preservation.

Fourth, if you grow herbs mainly for cosmetic purposes, it could be because you are conscious of the effect the mass production of modern cosmetics has on the environment. After all, factories belch out fumes to make face powder, and guar gum is shipped across the world to put into toothpastes and shampoos. And don't forget the well–publicized use of animals in laboratories for the testing of make–up, which is abhorrent to most people; it is, of course, something that would be abolished if we all used home–grown plants as bases for our cosmetics.

And fifth, if you grow herbs for household purposes, it is likely to be because you enjoy the challenge – and the prospect – of keeping home in a self–sufficient way.

If you do not grow herbs at the moment, but you are an organic gardener (or would like to be), then I can certainly recommend that you give herb cultivation a try. These plants are generally easy to grow, they are one of the few groups of plants that are generally free of pests and diseases and, depending on what you grow, they can improve the taste of food, provide useful medication and cosmetics, and serve other purposes in and around the home.

Tolerance to pests

Herbs usually have strong flavours or aromas, which come from aromatic or volatile oils and other substances in the plant including tannins, bitters, mucilages, alkaloids, saponins and glycoides. As well as making herbs useful plants, these substances are unpalatable

▽ **Even snails (one of the worst garden pests) tend to avoid the vast majority of herbs.**

to many of the traditional garden pests. Creatures from aphids to slugs, and from rabbits to deer, are known to avoid infesting or attacking many herbs. This means that the gardener does not need to apply so many pest–control products in order to keep the plants healthy and productive. This is music to the ears of the organic gardener.

There are, of course, a few pests and diseases that affect garden herbs, but these are much less significant and occur on a far smaller scale than, say, blight on tomatoes, which can devastate a crop, or caterpillars on cabbages, which require either labour–intensive vigilance or massive pesticide use. Environmentally friendly control measures for pests and diseases of herbs are considered on pages 78–83.

Tolerance of dry conditions

IN GENERAL, herbs come from parts of the world where the sun shines brightly and the soils are largely dry. India, China and the Mediterranean regions, in particular, are the natural homes of many of our most popular herbs. This means that the majority of herbs you might want to grow are undemanding and do not need gallons of precious water in summer. Thus herbs are not only well suited to organic, environmentally sustainable gardening but they are also perfect for people who don't have the time or inclination to do much labour–intensive gardening.

Contrast this with other popular summer garden plants, such as bedding plants and containers, or crops such as tomatoes, peppers,

▼ **Dry soils – this is a heavy, cracked clay soil during a drought – are frequently fine for herbs.**

cucumbers, celery, potatoes and runner beans: all of these types of plant need copious quantities of watering. Many herbs, by comparison, often thrive on near neglect.

Tolerance of poor soil

THERE IS a similar tale to tell in terms of the soil. Good organic gardeners usually have an endless supply of well–rotted, 'recycled' plant waste – or garden compost – and the instinct when planting is to liberally dose a hole with it to give the plant something nutritious and water–retentive to get its roots into. This, however, is not always necessary with herbs. The natural homes of many herbs are the arid and impoverished soils of scrubland. In fact, if you take a woody herb such as lavender and give it a highly nutritious, fertile soil with well–rotted compost at planting time, and regular doses of fertilizer over the first year, there is a very good chance that it will die. The mixture, in simple terms, would simply be too rich for it.

This means, particularly if the garden compost is in short or limited supply, that it can be used elsewhere to much better effect. Herbs in general, therefore, tend not to use as much of the gardener's natural resources as many other plants.

▼ **English lavender (*Lavandula angustifolia*) actually comes from northern Spain and will tolerate poor soil.**

Companion planting

IF MY garden vegetables and fruits succumb to pests and diseases they have two choices. They either pull through, or they die. It may sound like tough love, but I'd much rather plant out extra stock than have to apply a cocktail of toxic chemicals. One way to help prevent pests from attacking plants is to adopt 'companion planting'. This is where you plant different plants together, so that one can help improve the growth of the other.

Some plants can actually deter insect pests from attacking a valuable neighbouring plant, and if you manage to prevent insect attack the plants have more chance of surviving virus diseases. Normally you would achieve this by planting a strong-smelling plant next to a vulnerable plant, to attract the pest away from it. But you can also set out a plant to attract the predator of a certain pest as well. For example, you can plant marigolds around tomatoes, and roses to attract aphid-feasting hover flies.

Growing the following herbs is known to deter butterflies, moths, flies and beetles from laying their eggs on neighbouring plants: dill, borage, coneflower, elderberry, garlic, lavender,

▲ **Marigolds can be grown with tomatoes and aubergines to attract aphid predators and to deter whitefly.**

marigold, mint, rosemary, thyme and valerian. Clover is generally considered to be a weed of lawns, but when grown – on purpose – in, say, an orchard, it has real benefits. In fact, many fruit growers like to cultivate a patch of clover around the bases of their trees, as it attracts pollinating moths, flies, butterflies and beetles. It also attracts the codling moth, a major pest of apples, but the smell of the clover overpowers that of the apples (to which the moth would normally fly long distances).

Lavender is a good companion plant to roses. The latter are prone – as any rose grower knows only too well – to blackfly (or aphids). By planting a strong-smelling herb such as lavender next to the roses, the aphids will bypass them.

Another fine example of companion planting with herbs is the growing together of marigolds and lettuce. Slugs and snails love both plants, but they love marigolds far more. If you plant a sacrificial crop of marigolds, then with luck your lettuces will be left alone. In fact, I think it is a good idea to dot marigolds all around the garden – not for decoration, but to distract the slugs and snails, which when gathered in clusters around the marigolds, can be collected and disposed of by your own preferred method.

▼ **Growing borage close to vulnerable plants can be helpful, as it deters certain moths, butterflies and flies.**

△ **Aphids, such as these blackfly, are the scourge of many garden plants. However a row of summer savory will help keep them away.**

◁ **Flowers such as these calendula will help to attract pollinating insects to the vegetable garden.**

Garlic is great. Plant it around the base of a peach tree to help control the spread of peach leaf curl disease, and next to roses to entice them to produce a stronger perfume. Grow feverfew with carrots to help keep carrot fly away, and basil near to tomatoes to deter whitefly. A row of summer savory surrounding the broad (fava) bean patch will deter blackfly. It is said that chamomile, known as the 'plants' physician', can aid any sickly plant.

Rosemary planted with roses is said to keep the latter healthy, whilst a clump of Solomon's seal (*Polygonatum multiflorum*) planted with lily-of-the-valley (*Convallaria majalis*) is reputed to increase the size of the flowers, and to keep the general area healthy. Finally, try growing spearmint near roses to repel aphids, tansy near to fruit trees to repel insects, and hyssop near to cabbages to deter cabbage-white butterflies.

▽ **Feverfew is an attractive plant in its own right, and growing it with carrots will help keep carrot fly away.**

Bad companion planting

There are certain plants you should not grow together because either one is in competition with the other for the same nutrients, or one exudes naturally occurring chemicals that inhibit the growth of the other. Some examples of bad herb companions are:

• Sage and cucumber: the roots of newly germinated cucumber plants stop growing when they come into contact with volatile chemicals produced by shrubs like sage.

• Sweet basil and rue: both plants grow poorly if sited next to each other; this disharmony is made more interesting by the inherent nature of the two plants – basil is one of the sweetest of plants in terms of taste, whilst rue is one of the most bitter.

• Dill and carrots: dill is often sown in small quantities in the corner of the vegetable garden where it can be allowed to flower and attract honey bees; however, if carrots are nearby, the presence of flowering dill seems to reduce greatly the carrot crop.

Attracting wildlife

▲ **Many insects tend to avoid the herb garden, but bees happily search out the flowers, such as this *Echinacea*.**

HERBS ARE not generally known and grown for their appeal to most common forms of wildlife. As stated already, many herbs contain substances that insect pests find repulsive. Pennyroyal, rue and tansy, for example, repel ants; mint, mugwort, rue and southernwood repel flies; mint and tansy repel mice; sweet bay repels weevils; and burning dry leaves of hemp agrimony (*Eupatorium cannabinum*) drives away wasps.

To a degree, the repelling nature of many herbs will also drive away other forms of wildlife as well, and, if you think of the food chain, if insects are absent then so will be the many other creatures that consume them. So if you want a garden that attracts a wide diversity of wildlife, do not fill it with herbs.

However, if you plant carefully, you can have herbs that attract the 'right kind' of wildlife. Take bees, for example. You can keep bees and herbs in perfect harmony – and make your own honey into the bargain.

For the best nectar production and pollination, grow your herbs in full sun and plant in groups of five or more. Erect some form of windbreak if the site is not sheltered, or bees will be buffeted by the wind. A hedge of holly or ivy acts both as an effective windbreak and as a supplier of nectar flowers in spring and autumn. Clovers,

Did you know?

In a decorative (rather than functional) herb garden you will often find a 'bee skep'. This is a decorative bee 'house', usually conical in shape and made from braided straw. Traditionally skeps were used to keep bees, but they ceased to be popular when hives that could be opened to harvest honey were developed. The skep had to be destroyed during the gathering of the honey. However, siting a skep in a herb garden is pointless, since bees ignore plants – even nectar-rich plants – within a radius of about 50ft (15m) from the hive. This is because the area may be contaminated by the bees' own so-called 'cleansing flights': bees habitually defecate in their hives, so when the sun is shining and the temperature rises the bees will take a short cleansing flight, to shake off any dirt on them.

oil–seed rape, sainfoin, mustard, charlock, willow herb and dandelion are the most important nectar plants for bees, but lavender, rosemary, bugle, catmint, borage, thyme, *Echinacea*, catnip, hyssop, sage, fennel, valerian, marjoram and the mints are all favoured by honey bees. Select herbs that will provide nectar and pollen for the longest period.

Homemade fertilizers

As WELL as containing tannins, bitters, mucilages, alkaloids, saponins and glycoides, herbs are also rich in minerals. This cocktail of substances found naturally in the plants – as well as providing diversity and a valuable addition to our own diets – can be of nutritional benefit to other plants.

The best example of this is comfrey. This soft, large–leaved plant is particularly rich in potassium, which makes it ideal for feeding fruiting vegetables such as tomatoes and cucumbers as well as flowering bedding plants. It also makes a good general–purpose liquid fertilizer, rich enough to supply most plants with nutrients.

Although the common comfrey (*Symphytum officinale*) is suitable for this, a far better form, containing higher amounts of potassium, calcium, iron and manganese, is the hybrid Russian comfrey (*S. x uplandicum*). As well as its chemical attributes, this latter plant starts to grow earlier in the year, is more vigorous and offers a better crop for continuous cutting for the compost maker.

Compost activator

THE LEAVES also act as a good 'activator' for the compost heap. This is a substance that is applied to a heap to help it break down some of the less degradable subjects, such as dry leaves and thicker stems. Apply comfrey leaves directly to the heap – there is no need to add the comfrey 'feed' to the heap; in fact, this would be a waste of it. Commercially available activators often contain herbal extracts in order to work effectively: chamomile, dandelion, nettle, valerian and yarrow are common ingredients.

Actually, I would strongly recommend that any general waste, debris and clippings from herbs in general, not just comfrey, are put on to the compost heap, as this is the best way of recycling the valuable minerals they contain. Some may help to activate the heap, some strong-smelling ones may deter flies and some may even sweeten the smell for you as well.

▽ **Comfrey, with leaves rich in potassium, is grown by many organic gardeners purely as a natural fertilizer.**

1 Cut the desired amount of comfrey leaves from the plant right to the base.

2 Place the leaves loosely in a large bucket or water butt, breaking them up a little.

3 Top up the container with water. Tap water is fine, but rainwater is better.

4 Leave to ferment for two to four weeks, or until the mixture turns black. The warmer the weather at the time, the quicker the fermenting process will be.

5 The clear brown liquid that results can then be strained off. If you use a water butt, with a tap at the base, then it would be worth placing a gauze across the internal opening to prevent the exit hole from being blocked by decomposed comfrey leaf tissue.

A small amount of concentrated fertilizer can be made by packing leaves tightly into a bucket that has small seep holes pierced into the bottom. Weigh down the leaves with a brick and stand the bucket over another container. After a few weeks black, fermented 'juice' will slowly drop through the holes. Dilute this concentrate at the rate of 2–4fl oz per gal (12–25ml per litre).

Once you have decided to create an organic herb garden, you need to choose the best place to put it and decide which style suits your situation best: it can be formal, contemporary, or even a simple window box. You should always be able to find somewhere you can grow herbs.

Planning a herb garden

Where to grow herbs

THERE ARE various factors you need to think about to make your herb garden a success, such as the amount of sun the area receives, the type of soil, whether the site is sheltered or exposed and, finally, how accessible you want the garden to be.

▼ **Nearly all herbs are at their best when growing in a position in full sun.**

How sunny is the area?

IF YOU wish to grow sun–loving herbs such as thyme, rosemary and savory, at least part of the site should face towards the sun (facing south if you live in the northern hemisphere, or facing north if you live in the southern hemisphere). This is the most important consideration when deciding where to grow herbs, as the other factors are easier to change or improve.

Generally, plants that come from hot, sunny parts have relatively small, individual leaves – for example, lavender, rosemary and thyme. If you looked at the leaves of such plants under the microscope you would see that they frequently have very thick surface cell layers, to protect the fragile, chlorophyll–containing cells from intense light and heat.

Chlorophyll, the green pigment of plants, is the unique agent for the miraculous business of photosynthesis, in which plants feed on the sun's light. The three factors needed for photosynthesis are sunlight, water and carbon dioxide. Shortage of any of the three will slow the process down. This is why most plants grow better in sunlight than the shade.

Many herbs are variegated (think of thymes and sage) or have purple leaves (basils and sage). However, all plants have essentially green leaves: those with yellow or variegated leaves have large areas of green on them, and those with purple leaves are actually green underneath.

It follows, therefore, that if a plant has leaves that are deficient in chlorophyll (such as variegated plants, where the chlorophyll is confined to certain areas), it will have a problem growing in a low–light area. This manifests itself in the plant being less vigorous and possibly stunted, and very much a 'poor relation' to its all–green counterparts. Some variegated plants if grown in a shady place will 'revert' to being all–green.

How moist is the soil?

SOIL MOISTURE is crucial for all plants and herbs are no exception. The one thing that the majority of aromatic herbs dislike, particularly those from the Mediterranean region, is having 'wet feet'. For this reason, the greater part of the chosen site for your herb garden must be well drained, so if it is likely to become waterlogged in winter it is best avoided completely. The ideal site would be one that slopes slightly towards the sun. Between these two extremes you can compromise – in the main – by trying to improve the drainage. This can often be done simply by forking over the soil to the depth of two 'spits' (one 'spit' is the depth of a spade's blade). This will break up any compacted layers just beneath the upper level of topsoil.

For most herbs, you will need to understand their summer watering requirements. Few will need watering daily, except during particularly hot weather and most can stand going several days without it. Many herbs, especially the sun–loving types such as scented pelargoniums and the succulent *Aloe vera*, are tolerant of dryish soils.

◁ **The leaves of purple sage are essentially green, with an upper layer of purplish pigmentation.**

▲ **This screen made from bamboo canes pinned together gives an attractive backdrop, as well as valuable shelter.**

▲ **A trelliswork panel can be used both to screen an area and to accommodate appropriate climbing plants.**

How sheltered is the garden?

WIND PROTECTION is also important for a herb garden; cold spring winds can do more harm to tender plants than very low temperatures. Evergreen herbs such as rosemary and sweet bay are easily scorched by icy blasts of wind on winter and early–spring days. In summer a windy site means more work staking up the taller herbs and watering those herbs that have been blown dry in sandy soil.

Of course it is not just the plants that will appreciate a more sheltered site. The bees and butterflies that are attracted to the flowers will not come if the area is too windswept, and the herb garden should also be an enjoyable and relaxing place for you to sit.

The ideal is a site that already has house or garden walls to the east as well as on the side opposite the path of the sun – in order to trap the sun's warmth. If you don't have this, you can put up a screen on which you can grow climbing plants to create a feeling of seclusion, confine the perfumes of aromatic plants and reduce wind buffeting. This can also mask undesirable views and reduce outside noise. You can also provide some shelter, if necessary, by putting up low walls or fences or by growing herb hedges (rosemary and lavender being the popular choices for this).

What is the soil acidity level?

LIGHT, SLIGHTLY alkaline soil is best for most herbs. A heavy, clay soil tends to become waterlogged and a very rich soil causes the herbs to make lush growth in which the aromatic oils are less concentrated. Most soils, whether too poor or too heavy, can be improved with the right treatment but you should consider the time and effort involved when choosing the site.

The soil's level of acidity or alkalinity is measured by the concentration of hydrogen ions, and is expressed as 'pH', or 'percentage hydrogen'. The scale is divided from 0 to 14, including

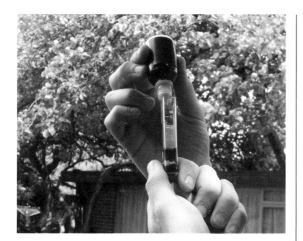

Use a pH testing kit from the garden centre to tell you the level of soil alkalinity or acidity in your garden.

PLANT FOOD			
pH	**N**	**P**	**K**
ALKALINE	Surplus	Surplus	Surplus
NEUTRAL	Sufficient	Sufficient	Sufficient
ACID	Adequate	Adequate	Adequate
VERY ACID	Deficient	Deficient	Deficient

Compare the colour of the completed test solution in the test tube against the colour chart supplied.

decimal placings. The 'neutral' point is pH 7.0. Figures above pH 7.0 indicate alkaline conditions; the higher the figure the more alkaline the soil conditions. The figures below pH 7.0 indicate acidity; the lower the figure the stronger the soil acidity is.

It is easy to test the acidity of the soil using one of the cheap pH test kits on the market. Although the pH level is not critical for growing herbs, many are native to alkaline territory. Therefore it is advisable to add lime to acid soils to bring the pH to 7.0, or just above, following the instructions in the kit. Herbs that prefer a slightly acid soil include parsley, rosemary, basil, chives, horseradish, sage and thyme.

How accessible is the site?

USUALLY THE best and most convenient place to have a herb garden is close to the kitchen door. It makes picking easier and avoids you having to traipse down the garden for one bay leaf. Also, having herbs growing close to an open window enables you to enjoy the aroma from the comfort of an armchair – especially on a warm summer's evening when scents are usually at their most powerful.

On the other hand, there is no point in trying to make a herb garden here if the conditions are not right for it. If your nearest suitable site is right down the end of the garden – or two miles away on an allotment plot – then that is where the herbs should be. In fact, there is some merit in creating a herb–garden retreat, far removed from the activities of the household.

In any case, even if you do have your main herb garden away from the kitchen, you could still grow some of your much–used favourites on the kitchen windowsill or in patio pots.

Your herbs should be easily accessible so that they can be gathered fresh – and quickly (even in bad weather).

Planning and design

HAVING CHOSEN the best site for your herb garden, you now come to arguably the most exciting stage – visualizing what the garden could look like, and putting this down on paper so that you have a template to work from. A well-planned design will make your herb garden a success right from the start.

Always match your idea to the constraints of the site and to the materials, time and expertise available. So before you even think about the plants you want to grow, you must consider the following: access paths, boundaries including walls, fences and herb hedges, and features such as an area for seating, a sundial, a scented arbour or a water feature.

It is worth making a plan on paper, as this helps you to overcome preconceived ideas based on what the site looks like now and enable you to explore completely new possibilities. Also, it is easy to fit curves and to draw and rub out lines as the design develops.

Measuring

MEASURE THE sides of the site and draw up the area on squared or graph paper, making each square represent a convenient measurement – such as 4in (10cm), 6in (15cm) or 12in (30cm). Start the measurements from a base line that is either parallel to your house or at right angles to it. Draw in clear, bold lines and mark in the main fixtures that are immovable: fences, buildings, trees and so on. Be as accurate as possible and note any changes of level that may require steps or raised beds.

Use overlays of tracing paper to try out different designs. Will your organic herb garden be formal, with geometric shapes, or informal, with irregular sweeps and curves? Try both, by drawing them on tracing paper and seeing which appeals to you most.

Establish the overall feel of a design before filling in any detail. Be prepared to discard lots of ideas before you find the one you like, and live with the idea for a few days before you make your decision.

◀ **Preparing a plan on paper helps you to overcome preconceived ideas of what the end result could look like.**

▼ **Before putting down ideas on paper you should measure the site, including boundaries and pathways.**

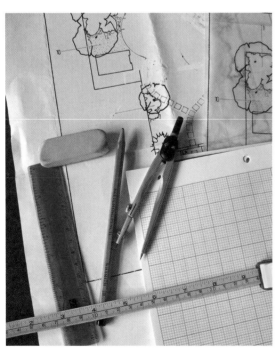

⚠ **Avoid laying a pathway straight through a site. This suggests rushing ahead; herb gardens are places to linger.**

Pathways

PATHS ARE important to the design of your herb garden because they introduce colour and patterns, and define its shape. The golden rule when it comes to pathways in herb gardens is that, for convenient access, plants should not be sited further than 30in (75cm) from the path. After all, you want to be able to get to the herbs for regular picking. This means that beds should be no more than 4–5ft (1.2–1.5m) wide, unless you insert stepping stones.

If possible, avoid putting a path straight through the centre of the space. It suggests rushing ahead, whereas a herb garden should

Be bold

If you want to create a modern, free-flowing herb garden, start with bold sweeping lines. New gardeners often tend to draw small, tight curves and these, when translated into three dimensions, can become exaggerated, i.e. tighter and far less practicable.

Grass alternatives

For those who want a green pathway in their herb garden, but consider grass to be too time-consuming, why not plant chamomile? It is a classic grass substitute and has been grown in this way for centuries. A lush, pale green creeping herb with small, feathery, aromatic leaves, it releases a pleasant fragrance when crushed underfoot. It is bruised easily, so would not survive heavy foot traffic. It may be found under either of its accepted Latin names: *Anthemis nobilis* or *Chamaemelum nobile*. The non-flowering variety 'Treneague' (below) is preferable as a grass substitute (as the daisy flowers of other varieties tend to spoil the carpeted effect). Use shears to clip back the straggly stems from time to time (see page 64).

be a place where you linger. To add interest, have a path change direction somewhere along its length, or break its flow by altering its pattern or colour in some way. You could try putting a piece of sculpture, or a tall herb, at a strategic place.

Adding interest is important, which is why you often see traditional and 'geometric' herb gardens with a chequerboard effect, frequently with alternate paving slabs missing.

Pathways can be of grass, but this can make mowing difficult and edging tiresome. If the paths are narrow or intricate, it is better to use bricks, blocks, paving slabs or gravel.

Walls and fences

A S STATED earlier, a herb garden should be sheltered, ideally making use of existing walls and fences. These can be used to support climbers appropriate to a herb garden such as vines, honeysuckle and blackberries. Scented climbing roses are always a good addition to a herb garden, but as an organic gardener you need to choose fairly disease–resistant varieties (see page 147).

If there are no existing walls, and you have sufficient space, you might consider building a low wall of brick or stone to act as a perimeter around the herb garden. If you want to build just one wall, however, this should be on either the exposed eastern side, or the side that will produce a sun–trap for your herbs.

▼ **This low hedge of variegated myrtle is being used to divide a vegetable plot from an adjacent herb garden.**

◄ **House walls can be maximized by strategically placing herb containers on and around them.**

Hedges and edges

A LTHOUGH THEY provide shelter, ordinary garden hedges make a less suitable surround for a herb garden than walls as they deplete the soil near to them. Also, large hedges do not show herbs off to their best advantage.

Some herbs themselves will make attractive hedges. Lavender, of course, is the most familiar. Old English lavender is the tallest type, growing to about 3ft (1m), and it provides some shelter for nearby low–growing herbs. Its flowers are striking for most of the summer, and it works particularly well if you want a long and straight hedge

Rosemary is also worth considering. However, it is more tender than lavender and would itself benefit from a sheltered position, so only consider this if you live in a mild area. Variegated myrtle, too, can be neatly trimmed into a low hedge.

In smaller herb gardens it is probably better to use bushy herbs to edge the beds. A dedicated or mixed row of salad burnet, parsley and chives can be very fetching. Alpine strawberries, too, make a fine edge.

▼ **This formal garden has a straight pathway, edged with box. The statue is a focal point at the end of the path.**

Traditional formal herb gardens

Formal designs in the garden depend on geometric shapes and straight lines; on regularity and symmetry. Balance is the key, usually with elements arranged around a central axis. A distinct pattern of paths, which form the structure, is all-important. These paths may be of brick, block, paving, gravel or grass, but make sure they are wide enough to walk on and to take a wheelbarrow.

Planting schemes follow the geometry of the layout, with corresponding blocks of colour filling the beds. Herbs grown for their attractive or useful leaves, especially those with a dense habit of growth, such as thyme, are often more suitable than those with a tendency to sprawl, whether or not they produce flowers and colour. Specimens of topiary, and plants growing over a shaped frame, are used in much the same way.

Ornaments, statues and large pots provide focal points at the ends of vistas. If placed to line a path edge or in a regular pattern, they will provide visual links, drawing the scheme together and reinforcing the regularity.

Sub-dividing a large border

A large border may be sub-divided by a pattern of internal clipped hedges for a more interesting effect. The spaces in between the hedges form individual planting areas – ideal for different species of herb. Tiling or timber edging could also be used.

Be understated

When planting up a formal garden beware of cramming in too much – for this look to be successful, understatement is best.

▼ **This formal herb garden is traditionally laid out, with beds and paths forming geometric patterns.**

▼ **In a large area, a formal herb garden can adopt the old English style of formality with impressive statuary.**

Informal herb gardens

INFORMAL HERB gardens can be made in many styles and adapted to suit the conditions in your garden. Designs based on fluid shapes and an irregular layout give plenty of scope for growing a variety of herbs. Actually, if your house and the surroundings are of a contemporary style, informal schemes usually fit better than formal ones.

Greenery and flowers can often be used to break up areas of hard material. Paths may be offset and gently curving, with beds and borders placed seemingly at random. Plants spill over onto the paths and spring up between cracks in the paving, or in amongst the pea shingle or gravel. Planting should be exuberant: large clumps of silver–leaved southernwood, forests of poppies or bergamot, stands of knapweed or evening primrose…the aim is to create a vibrant jumble of foliage and flowers.

The structure of the informal garden does not have to be completely irregular, however. A relaxed look is frequently achieved by the planting schemes as much as by the layout of beds and paths. This has its roots in the cottage–garden genre of gardening, in which a central path divided two rectangular areas and lack of space forced an eclectic mix of plants. A regular framework works well in many informal gardens, but it has to be simple – four rectangular beds,

▲ **This area of mixed planting contains a rich diversity of plants, set off by a mass of flowering thyme in the centre.**

divided by intersecting paths, perhaps. There is little room for complex patterns and rigid symmetry.

Mixed herb borders

IF THE overall garden is informal, your herbs may be best placed in mixed borders, along with perennials, shrubs, bulbs and temporary summer (bedding) plants. Remember, however, that this means your herbs will be spread around a wide area of the garden, which will almost certainly make gathering less easy.

▼ **Feverfew jostles for space with cotton lavender in this delightful yet informal setting.**

▼ **This water feature is backed by a collection of mauve and purple plants, including several different lavenders.**

Contemporary herb gardens

CONTEMPORARY HERB gardens are springing up in various places, and generally they are to be welcomed. However, whether you can truly say these contemporary gardens can be grown in an organic way, is debatable. The world's most famous show for fashionable gardening is the Chelsea Flower Show, held in London every May. It is the showcase for new plants, ideas and fashions and, as with the best of the catwalk shows, it sets trends. In recent years herbs have played a significant role in many of the more notable of Chelsea's gardens – but to many traditional gardeners (and especially those who are organically inclined) the herbs have been planted in incongruous ways.

Whole beds and borders, for example, have been planted with flowering thyme, and the gardener is encouraged to put down a blanket

Using plant mounds

Clipped mounds of plants such as box (the all-green, variegated or golden forms) or cotton lavender, may be used to great effect in any garden scheme (formal, informal or contemporary). Edging, hedging or 'dot' plants in low-planted carpet schemes – they can be very eye-catching.

over the thyme and to lay on it, to relax or even sleep there. It may be very comfortable, and the soporific aroma would certainly induce sleep.

Large blocks of colour, perhaps enhanced by some arching ornamental grasses, and edged with long lengths of perfectly trimmed box hedging, certainly looks delightful, and will be a talking point with friends.

Concrete paths, sheets of falling water, modern containers with single–colour plants all create this modern, contemporary feel. And if this is your choice, then I applaud your individuality, your design skill and your bravery at creating something different. But an organic herb gardener is a practical animal wanting variety, diversity and convenience all wrapped up in a sustainable way, with a carbon–footprint that is as low as can be achieved. Personally I do not believe that the organic gardening principle and contemporary garden design work particularly well together.

◄ **Modern wooden decking and grasses accompany a carpet of flowering thyme in a contemporary herb garden.**

Practical herb gardens

▲ Here, herbs have been planted amongst salad leaves and other quick-maturing vegetables.

◀ If you have just a small garden without room for a herb area, you may need to mix herbs with other plants.

OF COURSE most people do not have the luxury of space for a dedicated large herb garden with paths and statues and so on. If you have a small garden, perhaps a town garden or a courtyard, or even an average–sized suburban garden you will need something more practical.

You could either create a smaller dedicated area, or try mixing some herbs into a larger area – say a vegetable plot – or take them out of the garden environment completely and grow them on an allotment.

A herb wheel

A CLASSIC DESIGN that gives maximum accessibility to your herbs, and which takes up relatively little space, is the cartwheel. This was a feature of numerous Victorian gardens when old cartwheels (wagon wheels) were plentiful. They provide frameworks of little beds, with the spokes of the wheel forming the divider

▶ A herb wheel is a traditional and convenient way to grow and display herbs in a small space.

between one type of herb and another. In larger versions, paths form the spokes and the beds are the areas between them. The size of the wheel will be dictated by the amount of available space. A bed 15ft (5m) across will provide an excellent range of fresh herbs for cooking and salads, with

Plants for a herb wheel

Dill, coriander and parsley are fine herbs for a herb wheel but they all have issues. Dill and coriander have short life cycles, so you will need two or three sowings during the growing season to ensure a supply of young leaves. Parsley is a biennial plant – sown and grown one year for harvesting and drying the next. If you want a year-round supply, make two plantings, in early spring and again in late summer.

plenty to dry and freeze for winter use. When planting, it is a good idea to put in several plants of the same kind. This gives a mature look very quickly and ensures that there are plenty of harvestable herbs even after the first few weeks.

Allotments

WITH THE recent interest in growing–your–own, and the UK Government's advice to eat five portions of fruit and vegetables a day, allotment plots are enjoying a resurgence in popularity. Few are lying fallow – a complete contrast to the 1990s when they were being sold off for development through lack of use.

Traditionally, vegetable crops and fruiting plants are the staples of the allotment, but there is no reason at all why an area cannot be given

Did you know?

Allotments are usually measured in rods, poles or perches. They are all the same measurement – approximately 16½ft (5m).

over to herbs. With a standard allotment there is no question that there would not be space. As in the home garden, position the herbs where they are easy to pick: as plot edgers they are entirely appropriate and you will not have to muddy your boots to pick them in wet weather.

Kitchen gardens

IF YOU have room to grow vegetables, then there may also be room for a few herbs. If space is tight and you can only grow one or the other, I would like to put the case for herbs. They are generally more attractive than vegetables, particularly later in the summer when a vegetable plot looks very tired. Herbs have flowers of many colours, too, and lots are carried in free-flowering form – think of bergamot, borage, hemp agrimony and pot marigold. As you pass by a herb–filled kitchen garden your olfactory senses will be stimulated as well – herbs smell better than vegetables.

Where herbs cannot adequately compete with vegetables is in terms of the pure bulk of edible matter. You cannot, of course, harvest pounds/kilos of mint leaves as you would do the potatoes that traditionally go with them. But herbs do add that extra zing and zip to a meal, and, in my view, totally justify the amount of kitchen garden space you may give over to them.

▼ **Allotments can be perfect for herbs as, unlike vegetables, they don't suffer much in dry weather.**

Herbs in small spaces

THE RANGE of herbs that can be grown in a small space is wide, but you will need plenty of sunshine. If you have this and some space for containers, you will be able to grow almost anything. There are only a few herbs, such as horseradish (which needs a deep soil) and fennel (which produces lots of lanky top growth), that are not worth attempting in a container.

Windowsills

WINDOWSILLS ARE the perfect environment for extending your herb–growing season by sowing a wide range of annual herb seeds from mid–autumn through to late winter. Sowing at these times fools the seeds into thinking that spring has arrived. They will sprout, and fresh leaves and stems will be yours for the taking for three, four or five months.

Sow a couple of good pinches of seed in each of several different pots, cover with less than ½in (10mm) of compost, water (but not too much) and

cover the pots with a clear polythene food wrap. This traps the moisture so your plants won't dry out. Store the pots somewhere warm – with a consistent temperature of 18–20°C (64–68°F) – but not necessarily light; an airing cupboard would be an ideal place.

Germination times vary from one or two days for chives right up to six weeks for parsley. Check the pots every day and immediately move any that show signs of growth. Remove the wrap and place the pot on a bright windowsill. From this point on, light is all–important. Four to six hours per day of direct sunlight is preferable. Temperature fluctuations should also be avoided, so watch out for excessive heat from radiators or chilly drafts from open doors or windows.

As the seedlings mature, pluck out the weaker ones to give their stronger siblings more room to grow. These thinnings can also be eaten.

Amongst the most popular herbs for growing in this way are: basil, chives, coriander, parsley and rocket (and don't forget the sprouting seeds, such as mung beans and fenugreek, that can be grown on windowsills – but do not need any soil).

◀ **You can be creative with small areas; here a mixed planting is enclosed in attractive wattle fencing.**

▽ **Basil and chives are just two of the herbs that grow well on a windowsill; both need regular trimming and use.**

Herbs in containers

MY MOST valued of herbs – mint, basil, parsley, rosemary and coriander – are all grown in containers close to the kitchen door. However, container herbs can be useful elsewhere in the garden, too. As part of a garden scheme, containers can be placed as a focal point, arranged symmetrically to link different elements of a design, or put into a bed to fill a temporary bare patch.

Window boxes

THESE CAN be perfect for bringing extra convenience to your herb growing – just open the window and pick. Window boxes can be rested on sills if those on the building are large enough, or they can be fixed to the wall below windows.

Boxes are available in various sizes, and you can also buy sets consisting of the box, a water tray to avoid dripping and the brackets for fixing to the wall. Plastic is the lightest material and wood is the most natural and practical material.

Many of the culinary and aromatic herbs are ideal for window boxes. Try chives, parsley, golden creeping lemon thyme, basil (if the

▼ **Many herbs are ideal for window boxes, even more so if the box is in a sheltered position.**

△ **Herbs in pots are best kept close to the kitchen door, but they can brighten up any dull part of the garden.**

position is sheltered) and even a small rosemary. A pot marigold (*Calendula*) adds cheerful colour and flower petals for salads and rice dishes. Another flower for eating is the bright orange–red nasturtium, which also provides trailing stems to hang attractively from the window box. If the box is sited in a hot, dry place, try the saffron crocus (*C. sativus*) for its valuable crop. The planting process for herbs in window boxes is the same as for planting a patio tub (see page 66).

Pot mobility

Remember that very large pots, or those made of stone or concrete, will be heavy – possibly too heavy to move. But, unlike static planting in a bed or border, medium-sized and smaller pots, or those made of a lighter material such as plastic, can be moved around as required. This is also useful for plants that have gone over, which need a less prominent position in which to recover. Also, tender and half-hardy herbs in pots can be moved under cover when the weather cools at the end of the growing season.

Hanging baskets

EVEN IF you don't have a garden, there will still be room for a hanging basket outside a window or on a balcony: there is no excuse not to grow herbs.

There are a number of different basket types available. The wire basket is the traditional type; the soil within it is kept in place using a basket liner. Sphagnum moss was the traditional material used for lining hanging baskets as it was lightweight, looked natural and was readily available. Although you can occasionally still find this, it is frowned upon by organic and sustainable gardeners as harvesting sphagnum depletes its natural habitat, harming wildlife. These days man–made fabric liners in green, brown or black do the job just as well.

There are also plastic baskets with filled–in sides available, and in many ways these are easier to manage. To start with, they dry out less quickly and some types have a built–in water reservoir or tray to save on watering. Make sure that the plastic basket you choose has holes in the side for trailing plants to be positioned.

Herbs for a hanging basket

Choose herbs that suit the shape of the basket. Go for plants that produce arching or trailing stems, or whose leaves grow in horizontal mounds or layers. Avoid upright plants. The following herbs will all work well.
Full sun: catmint, prostrate winter savory, creeping thymes, basil, prostrate sage and prostrate rosemary.
Part-shade: parsley, pennyroyal, chives, variegated mint, periwinkle and nasturtium.

Thymus 'Archer's Gold'

Take care not to site hanging baskets between tall buildings where strong wind tunnels often form, causing damage to delicate herbs. The planting process for herbs in hanging baskets is described on page 65.

Patio tubs

THESE ARE, of course, ideal for standing on a patio, path, driveway or next to a door. But they can also look very good when stood in borders. The tubs, raised slightly on blocks, can be placed for convenience when the herbs in the tub are at their peak for picking.

◀ **The best herb hanging baskets are those in which the herb shapes are sympathetic to the basket.**

⚠ **Bronze fennel is grown for effect in this modern square metal pot but is not usually recommended for containers due to its ultimate height.**

There is a wide range of tubs available, made from wood, plastic, terracotta, reconstituted stone and moulded resin. The plastic ones are the cheapest but some are rather garish, so look for those that are not too obtrusive. The most popular colours for plastic are white, green and brown. See page 66 for how to plant a tub with herbs.

Herbs for patio tubs and troughs

Basil, borage, catmint, coltsfoot, chamomile, chives, clary, lemon balm, lungwort, mint (particularly the round-leaved kinds), parsley, tarragon, thyme and violet.

Lemon balm (*Melissa officinalis*)

Bay watch

Sweet bay (*Laurus nobilis*) is one of the most popular choices for patio tubs, and it is often clipped to a formal shape. It saves time to purchase these already trained, but half the fun is creating the feature yourself. With care they can be expected to last for many years. Cold winds are the chief enemy of these potted trees, and if you live in a cold or exposed position they will appreciate being moved into a porch or light hallway, or even a conservatory, during winter.

Controlling mint

Mint (*Mentha* spp.), generally, is a most invasive herb. When planted outside in the garden soil it can take just two years before you regret the move. In that time the underground 'stolons' can stretch throughout the bed or border, and into lawns and driveways and under patios. For this reason, I only ever grow mint in containers, where I can keep them under control.

Propagating your own plants is not only a cheap way to stock your garden, it is also one of the real joys of gardening. There are few better feelings than to see a haze of green as you view your recently sown trays and pots, or to discover that a cutting you didn't hold out much hope for has actually produced a handful of healthy roots. Many herbs will grow from seed and a large proportion can also be grown from cuttings and division.

Propagating herbs

Sowing seeds

Annual and biennial herbs must be raised from seed, and some perennial types can also be increased in this way. However, be aware that herb seeds can sometimes be slow to germinate, are often incredibly tiny and may require certain special conditions such as very high temperatures, light, or a period subjected to frost or freezing temperatures. Also, for some herbs, very fresh seed is required, so if you buy packets of seed from garden centres you will be at an immediate disadvantage.

Outdoor sowing

Those herbs that are both hardy and either annual or biennial can be sown outdoors directly in garden beds. These plants usually become leggy if sown indoors in pots or trays, and they have a tendency to bolt (flower and run to seed prematurely) when they are transplanted.

▼ **Sowing herb seeds is easy and satisfying, especially if you are able to collect them from your own crops.**

Sowing requirements

Annual herbs needed in quantity, such as parsley and dill (for dill seed) can be sown in a row in the vegetable garden. Others, such as rocket (below) and chervil, need only a small patch in the herb garden. In this case scatter some seed over the soil surface and then bury most of it by raking gently in all directions. Some perennial herbs, including fennel, seed themselves all over the garden.

1 Start by preparing the soil well. Dig it over and remove any weeds. It is not generally advisable to incorporate well-rotted manure or compost for seed-sown herbs – it tends to be too rich for them.

2 Shuffle your feet over the dug area in order to expel most of the air pockets created by the digging, and then use a rake to level the area and remove stones and other debris. A finer rake will then enable you to create a fine 'tilth' – a crumbly 1in (2.5cm) surface to the soil.

3 This is the perfect medium in which to make a shallow drill – with a hoe, or corner of a rake – alongside a taut string attached to two markers. Generally, the drill should be between ¼–½in (6–13mm) deep; the larger the seed, the deeper it can usually be set. Then water the drill using a watering can with a fine rose-end attached. Sow the seeds thinly – two or three per 1in (2.5cm) of drill is plenty. Then cover the drill gently with soil and lightly firm the surface.

As long as the seeds were good, and there is moisture and air with some warmth, then they will germinate. Generally, the higher the temperature is, the quicker the germination. Early to late spring, and late summer to early autumn are the main sowing periods for herbs.

When the seedlings have emerged, and they are large enough to handle, some should be removed gently so that the remainder stand clear of each other. This thinning will also need to be repeated when the young plants become fully established.

Indoor sowing

▲ **Herbs grown from seed sown indoors must be 'hardened off' outside before being planted in the garden.**

By SOWING seeds indoors (greenhouse, garden frame, conservatory or kitchen windowsill) it is far easier to give them the ideal conditions – mainly warmth and consistent moisture – for germination.

It is very important to use the right compost when sowing seeds indoors. The soil–based (John Innes) composts usually contain chemical fertilizers, and so are not organic. Likewise,

the use of peat in many shop–bought soil–less composts is not something that a truly organic and sustainable gardener would wish to use. Fortunately, herb seedlings do not require much in the way of feeding, so a good solution is to mix your own compost with two parts coir compost to one part coarse horticulture sand. I tend to water coir compost a day or two before sowing, using a liquid seaweed fertilizer (diluted to the manufacturer's instructions for seedlings).

1 Small individual pots are fine for sowing just one or two plants. Fill them to the brim with the compost mix, then level it off and press the surface flat. Sow a pinch of seeds onto this surface. Large seeds (such as parsley and coriander) can be 'space–sown', that is, three or four seeds spaced across the surface of the compost. If the seeds are tiny it is not necessary to cover them with any more compost, but if they are larger, then put a little of the compost into a coarse sieve and shake it to give them a light covering. Stand the pots in a shallow tray of water until the moisture seeps right up through the compost, then take them out and stand them on normal greenhouse staging (or a dry saucer if indoors). An average temperature of 60°F (15°C) is usually about right for most herb seedlings to germinate successfully.

2 When the seedlings are large enough to handle, thin them out to a larger pot or tray, to prevent overcrowding. Fill the new container with a peat–free compost and make holes in it.

3 Hold each young seedling by a leaf rather than by its stem and, using a dibber, prise it carefully out of the compost to avoid breaking or bruising its fragile new stems and roots.

4 Put the seedling in the hole, dangling the roots into it and then gently closing it by pushing in soil with your fingers. Label the tray.

5 Site the container in a light place away from direct sunlight. Check daily, moving the container and watering the plants as necessary.

Taking cuttings

THERE ARE three main types of stem cutting suitable for herbs: softwood (from new shoots that have not yet hardened), semi-ripe (from new growth when it has started to firm up at the base) and hardwood (from woody shrubs and trees). There are also root cuttings (taken from small pieces of root, which are more applicable to some plants than others).

Stem cuttings

FOLLOW THE same basic technique for all three types of stem cutting. Softwood cuttings should be sturdy 2–4in (5–10cm) long pieces with plenty of leaves; semi-ripe cuttings could be a little longer – up to 6in (15cm) – and hardwood cuttings are generally longer still at 6–15in (15–38cm) long.

Semi-ripe cuttings of rosemary

The photographs on the facing page show semi-ripe cuttings of rosemary (*Rosmarinus officinalis* 'Miss Jessop's Upright') being taken. This technique applies just as well to all of the plants in the softwood and semi-ripe lists (page 52).

Choose healthy, vigorous shoots without flower buds or signs of disease or pests. Using a clean, sharp knife, take each cutting from just below a leaf node; this is where growth cells congregate in the stem and is the place on the cutting from where roots will eventually emerge. Try to make all cuts cleanly and without ragged edges, as this can result in non-rooting or provide entry points for bacteria or fungi. Strip away the leaves from the lower third, taking care not to tear the stem.

Most herbs root well without the need for hormone rooting powder or gel but with difficult plants such as sweet bay (*Laurus nobilis*), it is pretty much essential. You can buy organic rooting powders but in my experience their effectiveness has been patchy – so I actually prefer the cautious use of traditional powders and gels. I feel I can justify their use in that by successfully propagating my own plants I am reducing the plant miles (transportation of green plant material), and the energy needed in the relatively intensive nursery production of plants for retail. To use rooting powder, dip the very base of the cutting in the substance and then tap off any excess.

◀ **Taking stem cuttings of woody herbs is an inexpensive way of increasing stock, and is not difficult if the proper procedure is followed.**

1 Select material from the current season's growth. Choose healthy, blemish-free stems. Each cutting should be removed from the parent plant with a clean cut made just below a bud, and should be kept moist and in the shade until you can prepare it.

2 Back in the greenhouse or potting shed, use a sharp, clean knife to prepare the cuttings. The best cutting length is 2–6in (5–15cm).

3 Remove leaves from the lower third to half of the cutting; if left, these will rot just under the surface of the compost and may attract disease. Most herbs root well without the need for hormone rooting powder or gel.

4 Fill a plant pot or tray containing a standard peat-free cuttings compost, or make your own mixture with equal parts moist sand and coir. Then insert the cutting about 1in (2.5cm) deep. If putting in more than one cutting, do not set them closer than 3in (7.5cm) apart. Label them and water them in well.

5 For individual pots of cuttings, cover with a clear plastic bag to maintain humidity around the stems and leaves, and moisture in the compost. The plastic bag should be clear or white, to allow good light transmission. Seal the bag in place by stretching an elastic band around the circumference of the pot. The kitchen windowsill (or greenhouse if you have one) will be an ideal place to keep it until roots have formed, but keep it out of direct sun.

6 The length of time it takes before the cutting is rooted will depend on humidity, air and soil temperature, and moisture availability around the forming roots. As a guide, it should take between 5 and 25 weeks. If semi-ripe cuttings taken between mid-summer and mid-autumn have not 'taken', and formed at least a few good roots, within 25 weeks, they are unlikely to take at all.

Protection for cuttings

SOFTWOOD CUTTINGS normally root in a greenhouse or on a kitchen windowsill (covered with a plastic dome or bag as described on page 51). These are tender cuttings and will need protection.

A garden frame or cloche is a good place to root semi-ripe cuttings. If your garden soil is sandy and free-draining, you may be able to root cuttings directly into the ground. If your soil is heavy or wet clay, place the cuttings in pots or trays, and then place these into the frame or under the cloche.

The frame should be kept closed for the first few days, but ventilate if the temperature climbs above 75°F (24°C). On average, semi-ripe cuttings take 5–25 weeks to root after insertion.

Root cuttings

THIS IS a good way to propagate mint, comfrey and horseradish. Take pieces of root 2–3in (5–7.5cm) long, and then lay them along the surface of potting compost in a seed tray. If the roots are bent, you may like to pin them in place with pieces of wire, so that the majority of the root length is in contact with the compost.

Thicker-rooted cuttings, such as comfrey, can be inserted vertically into the compost. Push them in so that they are entirely buried, and then cover the compost surface with a ¼in (6mm) layer of sand to help prevent the compost from drying, as well as to maintain darkness for the roots.

▼ **Mint is best propagated by taking cuttings of the roots and laying them on the surface of a cuttings compost.**

Herbs for cuttings

All woody herbs can be grown from cuttings, but those listed here are generally the easiest.

Softwood
Catnip/catmint, lemon verbena, marsh mallow, curry plant, hyssop, lavender, lemon balm, mint, pelargonium, rosemary, sage, santolina and thyme.

Semi-ripe
Balm of Gilead, bergamot, curry plant, horehound, hyssop, lavender, lemon balm, marjoram/oregano, mint, myrtle, pelargonium, rosemary, rue, sage, santolina, sweet bay, tarragon (French), thyme, winter savory and wormwood.

Hardwood
Elder, roses (ramblers) and santolina.

Root cuttings
Bergamot, comfrey, horseradish, lovage, marjoram/oregano, mint and mullein.

Heel cuttings

Stem (soft, semi or hardwood) cuttings from woody plants were traditionally taken by pulling a shoot away from the main stem in order to retain a small sliver of bark, or a 'heel'. This heel contains higher levels of growth hormones (known as 'auxins'). This method is useful for plants with pithy stems, aged plants or those in bad condition.

Dividing and layering herbs

Dividing perennial herbs

THIS SIMPLY means taking a plant and dividing it into smaller plants that can be grown on to become mature plants just as the 'parent' had been. After just a few years many herbs can grow into quite sizeable clumps. The more vigorous plants are likely to start deteriorating after this time, as the shoots become overcrowded and the centres of the clumps get 'woody'. Therefore dividing plants into smaller pieces not only increases the stock of them, it will also give them an entirely new lease of life.

Autumn and spring are the best times to undertake division. Dig up the plant and remove old flower stems. Carefully separate the plant into individual sections, each with a growing point and some roots. Clumps of bulbous plants, such as chives, can be pulled apart, with thumbs pressed into the centre of the clump and opened

A knife is being used to divide this overgrown clump of marjoram. Each cut section can then be replanted.

out. With tougher plants you can use an old kitchen knife to cut across the crown. Larger plants should be divided by inserting two garden forks back–to–back and prising them apart. Use a garden spade to chop through a large clump, but there is a risk that you will cut through important growth buds.

Herbs for dividing

Bistort, chives, cowslip, elecampane, Good King Henry, lawn chamomile, lemon balm, lovage, lungwort, marjoram, meadowsweet, primrose, pyrethrum, sorrel, Sweet Joe Pye, sweet violet, tansy, tarragon, thyme, wall germander and wormwood.

Herbs for layering

Clove pink, lavender, mint, rosemary, sage, sweet bay and thyme.

Layering herbs

THE AIM of layering is to encourage sections of plant to root while still attached to the parent plant. This is how many shrubby plants spread in the wild. For the home gardener it is used in cases where cuttings prove difficult to root.

If the soil under the plant is heavy, add sand or peat-free compost. Bend a sturdy, flexible stem to the ground. 'Scrape' it with your fingernail, or sandpaper, at the point where it touches the soil, and then peg or weigh it in place. Bury the stem by heaping soil over it, making sure that the area in contact with the soil is not exposed. After several months little roots will have formed, and you can separate the new shoot from its parent. Pot it up or move straight to the garden.

As well as garden centres, there are specialist nurseries and mail-order suppliers – all offering a range of enticing herbs to try. In fact, the choice of herbs that are available is enormous, and the different ways to buy and plant them can be bewildering to a beginner.

Buying and planting herbs

Buying herbs

ONCE YOU have decided on a herb garden, and have maybe even identified which plants you want to grow, you will need to go out and buy them. When choosing any herb from a shop, garden centre or nursery, look for healthy specimens. There should be no weeds, or pests or diseases. Let's look at the key herb plant groups.

Annual and biennial herbs

ANNUALS ARE plants that are sown, grow, flower and die all within a year, whereas biennials are sown and grown on in one year, and flower and die during the second year. Some of the most popular annual and biennial herbs are listed on page 166.

In the case of annual herbs, the plants should not be flowering. If they are, they will have used up and wasted their energies and could be stressed. If the plants you desire have all started to flower whilst still on the shop's shelves, go for the trays, or plants, with the fewest flowers.

Perennial herbs

THESE ARE plants that, although not woody, will survive and be useful to you from year to year. Familiar perennial herbs are listed on page 166.

Perennial herbs are nearly all sold in pots (the exception is when you are buying by mail order; roots are wrapped in moist compost or other material to be sent out). It is worth buying the best plants you can, so look for vigorous, healthy specimens that are young, as these will tend to establish and grow quickly. Don't necessarily buy the largest plants, though, as these may be pot-bound and will take time to establish. If you do end up buying a perennial herb that is pot-bound, gently tease out as many of the roots from the congested 'ball' of root as possible before planting, but try not to damage them.

Shrubby and climbing herbs

SHRUBS IN general form the backbone of a garden and without them a garden would appear unusual – everything would be low down, and stems and foliage would be soft and wavy; there would be no firm 'substance' to the garden. The same can be said of shrubby herbs in a herb garden. Some of the best-known shrubby and woody climbing herbs include cotton lavender, curry plant, elder, lavender, lemon balm, marjoram/oregano, myrtle, roses (climbers and ramblers), rosemary, sage, sweet bay and wormwood.

Most shrubby and climbing herbs will be found growing in pots at the garden centre, but try to make sure that they are genuine container-grown plants, not bare-root specimens that have recently been potted up, perhaps hurriedly, to make a quick sale. You can tell if shrubs have been in their containers for the proper length of time by moss or algae on the soil surface. Another way to identify how long a plant has been in a pot is to see if the roots are beginning to push through the holes in the base of the pot.

Some woody plants – mainly trees, but some shrubs and frequently climbers – are sold as 'bare-root' plants (where they have been grown in the ground at the nursery rather than in pots). These are usually sold in smaller plant nurseries, through mail-order plant businesses and in stores and supermarkets. In the case of the latter two, these bare-root plants are prepacked and sealed, usually with some moisture kept around the roots by packing them in moist tissue paper, or a small amount of compost.

If you really know what you are looking for, it is possible to get excellent plants in this way, and they are usually cheaper than container-grown types because you are not buying the pot and soil. You also have the advantage of seeing if the plant has a well-developed root system.

Beware, however, of those with wrinkled, dried-up stems, or premature growth caused by high temperatures in transit, or in the shop, where the transparent packaging has created a mini 'greenhouse' around the plants. Saleable plants should have a good, fibrous root system and a minimum of two strong, firm shoots, no thinner than a pencil, and preferably thicker.

Specialist herb nurseries offer the widest possible range, but always make sure you look for quality, too.

Sourcing plants

Visit a nursery

SPECIALIST HERB nurseries are the best place to buy herbs. Visiting the nursery in person enables you to see the herbs before you purchase them, but more than this, it allows you to talk to the growers. These specialists enjoy talking about their plants, and it is in their interests to encourage you to try new varieties and to get the best out of your hobby.

Go to a garden centre

HERBS CAN usually be bought from your local garden centre, but the range of species and varieties offered is severely limited, and in many cases the treatment and quality of the plants leaves much to be desired. These retail outlets do not employ specialist staff, so do not expect detailed, one-to-one advice on herbs. General garden centres are, however, useful for novice herb gardeners, as plants are often less

Plants by post

Mail order plants are normally only sent out during the spring and autumn – the traditional times for planting and potting. If you are going away on holiday, even for just a few days, make sure you have a back-up plan for receipt of the plants. If they are left in a parcel for a long time you may be met with the sight of a rotting mass when it is opened. Either delay ordering your plants, arrange for a neighbour to open the delivery, or inform the company that you will be away between certain dates.

expensive, and the selection being offered is usually the easier-to-grow and frequently more popular types.

Mail order or internet

MOST OF the best specialist nurseries provide a catalogue of their stock. These are always worth getting hold of since they not only tell you what is available and how to order it, but they often give useful growing information as well. When buying plants by mail order you obviously do not see the plants before they arrive, but most reputable nurseries can be trusted to send out good plants. Increasingly nurseries also have their own websites with free online catalogues for you to view.

◀ **The benefit of visiting a specialist nursery over buying by mail order is that you can see what you are buying.**

Soil preparation

WHETHER YOU have propagated your own herbs using the methods described in Chapter 3, or you have bought plants from one of the sources described in this chapter, sooner or later you will need to plant them out. But before you do this, make sure that the soil has been properly prepared.

Bulky organic matter

DIG THE soil over and remove the weeds. In the case of long-lasting herbs, such as woody rosemary, roses, myrtle and sweet bay, you should dig in some bulky organic matter such as well-rotted compost or farmyard manure. It has to be well rotted, for if it rots while in the ground it can deplete the nearby soil of much-needed nitrogen.

Organic matter improves the texture and fertility of the soil, and eventually decomposes into beneficial humus (complete decayed organic matter). The addition of such material

is recommended for many soil types, including clay, where it helps to open up the sticky soil, so improving the drainage of rainwater. Conversely, organic matter also helps free-draining soils such as sands, gravels and chalk, to hold on to moisture and plant foods, since it acts like a sponge.

Manure is the best material if you want to feed the soil and increase its moisture-retaining capabilities. Manure from pigs and horses is most commonly available, usually from farms that put up signs. Sometimes a town-based garden centre will be able to order it in for you. It is not particularly expensive. Poultry manure is also available, but this is very strong and needs to dry out and be used as a fertilizer dressing rather than manure. Incorporate it at a rate of at least one level barrowload per 4sq yd (3.3m^2).

Apart from manure and homemade compost there are other forms of bulky organic matter. Coir, which is the fibre from coconut husks and is similar in appearance and texture to sphagnum moss peat, retains moisture well. It was used in gardening 150 years ago but it never became really popular, presumably because peat was accepted as the better soil improver.

Pulverized or shredded bark can be added to the soil during digging. It should, however, be partially composted and it should state this clearly on the bag. The benefit of this is that when it degrades further in the soil it will not deplete the soil of nitrogen. Bark is especially good at improving the drainage of, and opening up, heavy clay soils.

Peat should not be used. Created from decomposed ancient sphagnum moss and sedges extracted from bogs, it is often recommended as a soil improver, but it has little in the way of nutritional content and, more pertinent in this day and age, it is non-sustainable.

◁ **Homemade compost, a mixture of your own garden waste, is one of the best soil improvers around.**

▲ **When applying manure or compost to the soil, make sure it is well rotted and not fresh, or it can harm the soil.**

Improving drainage

HERBS HATE having their roots in a cold, wet soil – and if they get waterlogged in winter, most herbs will not recover. If you have a clay soil, you will know that after winter rains it becomes a sticky quagmire, and in the heat of the summer it bakes hard like concrete. Neither condition is conducive to good plant growth, so adding one of the bulky organic matters discussed on the previous pages will do wonders, particularly over a period of time.

If your garden soil is clay, and especially if the site is level, it will be necessary to dig a few deep sump holes and to fill them with some form of rough drainage, such as broken stone, brick or large–grade gravel, so that surplus moisture can soak away. On a sloping site, provide drainage by digging a few channels downhill and fill these with similar materials.

▶ **Silver plants, such as this wormwood (*Artemisia* 'Powis Castle' AGM), are less tolerant of wet soils.**

Coarse sand and grit

If you dig in a 2in (5cm) layer of coarse sand or grit some 8in (20cm) below the surface of a clay soil, it will open up the soil and allow rainwater to drain through more easily and swiftly. Both types are obtainable in bulk from builders' merchants, or in smaller bags from garden centres.

Planting in garden beds and borders

▲ **When planting, the hole should be the same size as the pot containing the young herb plant.**

◀ **Before planting, apply an even dressing of a good organic fertilizer (such as bone meal).**

BEFORE PLANTING remove any weeds that may have sprung up since the area was dug. To get the herbs off to a good start, apply a dressing of bone meal fertilizer over the area at the rate of 2oz per sq yd (65g per m²). Work it into the surface of the soil, using a hoe or rake, tread the area firm, and then rake it level.

Annual and biennial herbs

GIVE THE plants a thorough watering whilst still in their containers, pots or trays. Do this an hour or two before planting them, so that they are not stressed prior to the move. If the herbs are in individual pots, take them out gently and place them in a hole dug with a trowel. The hole should be the same size as the pot. Firm them in place with your hands, and water them in.

Sometimes young herb plants come in plastic or polystyrene strips; you will need to either break the strips apart or to gently tease the plants out of their compartments. Transplant them carefully; damaged leaves will be replaced with new leaves within reason, but a plant only has one stem so avoid causing it harm.

Perennial herbs

WITH PERENNIAL herbs, dig a hole that is large enough to accommodate the entire root system. Depending on the size of the plant, this will require using a trowel or a spade. Carefully remove the plant from its container

▼ **Water young plants well before planting so that they are not stressed prior to being set in the ground.**

▲ **Control weeds by planting herbs in fabric mulching material. Cut a hole (left), and set the plant within it (right).**

▲ **Disguise mulching fabric by covering it with a neutral organic substance, such as bark chippings.**

and, if possible, spread out the roots as you place the plant in the hole. Set the crown of the plant at soil level, then backfill, firm and water in the plant.

Why digging is important

Just because a container-grown plant has a neat root-ball when removed from its pot, do not be fooled into believing that planting involves simply dropping it into a hole. On a heavy, clay soil you would be inadvertently creating a sump from which water would be slow to drain, and this could cause the roots to rot. This is why digging the whole planting area is important. Or, at the very least, aim to break up the surrounding soil and the base of the hole at planting time, before firming the herb in position and watering it in.

Shrubby and climbing herbs

CONTAINER–GROWN SHRUBBY herbs and climbers can be planted at any time of year, but if you are planting in summer, or during a period of hot weather in spring or autumn, you must make sure to check for watering, almost on a daily basis, until the soil is consistently moist.

Late autumn is the ideal time for planting bare–root plants, and this is when nurseries and garden centres will be stocked to capacity with them. Setting a climbing plant against a wall usually requires you to plant it 12in (30cm) away from the wall, in order to avoid the footings.

Hardening off

Herbs you have propagated inside need to be acclimatized to outdoor conditions before being planted out. Start by standing them out all day in a sheltered position and bring them in at night. Then, a few days before planting – assuming the weather is mild – leave them out day and night. After this 'hardening-off' period, which should take about seven to ten days, the herbs should be planted out, but not until all danger of frosts has passed.

Planting herbs in paving

ALTHOUGH A herb garden is the ideal environment, herbs can be grown in a variety of other situations in the garden, including cracks and crannies in paving. Here are the conditions many small but useful herbs need: their heads should be in the light, whereas their roots should be in cool, moist soil beneath the paving stones. These same stones will also protect the herb stems and leaves from wet soil. Such plants are good for breaking up the hard lines of an 'unnatural' paved area. However, this will not work if the paved area is low–lying and sunless, and if it is prone to collecting large puddles after rainfall.

Suitable herbs for paved areas are usually low–growing mat– or small clump–formers, but do not be afraid to put in the occasional upright or small sub–shrub; these are semi–woody plants that are not particularly herbaceous or perennial in nature, yet survive for many years, such as cotton lavender.

In paths and paving where slabs have been laid, it is commonplace to remove one here and there or, in a more extreme way to remove alternate slabs in order to create a chequerboard

Herbs for paving

Plants that are good for using in paving are: chamomile, feverfew, hyssop, lady's mantle, lavender (dwarf), pellitory, pennyroyal, pinks, santolina, sedums, sempervivum, soapwart, thyme and wall germander.

effect. Planting in the places vacated by the slabs is fairly straightforward. More difficult is planting a herb to go in the cracks between irregular paving (or 'crazy paving').

You will not succeed if you try to push a plant's roots down into a crevice – you will do more harm than good to the plant. Instead you will need to lift one of the laid stones and to plant the herb, as close to a neighbouring stone as possible, and then re–lay the lifted slab. This is all dependent, of course, on there being a sufficient gap between the stones so that the plant can be placed without being damaged.

◀ **A variety of mixed herbs (including lady's mantle, golden feverfew and various *Artemisia*).**

▽ **Herbs can be planted in paving (left), but will often self-sow, as with this golden feverfew (right).**

Planting a herb lawn

SEVERAL DIFFERENT herbs can be planted to create a fragrant lawn 'carpet'. It is particularly nice to make a 'rug' in front of a garden seat, or a welcoming 'mat' as you enter the herb garden.

Start with a small area as all herb lawns involve a lot of ongoing weeding (although you will save time in the long–run as they do not generally need mowing). Weed the area thoroughly to remove every trace of perennial weeds, then rake the soil to a smooth surface. If the area is in full sun, plant Roman or perennial chamomile – with its apple–scented leaves – at 4in (10cm) intervals. 'Treneague' is the non–flowering clone; this is more convenient for a lawn as it saves having to remove flower heads.

▲ *Chamaemelum nobile* 'Treneague' is a flowerless herb whose fragrance wafts up when walked upon.

Sowing chamomile seed

You can create a chamomile lawn by sowing seed rather than planting – but you will need to sow seed of the Roman chamomile species. Dig and weed the area, and rake it to a fine tilth. Sprinkle the seed over the area, and then cover it with a thin, even layer of soil; this is best done by sieving the soil over the top of the seed. Keep the area moist.

When the seedlings have at least two sets of leaves, thin the plants out so they are about 3in (8cm) apart. Do not walk on them until they have started to bind together. Remove most flowers to encourage leaf vigour. However, I like to allow the odd flower as I think they add to the charm of the lawn.

However, the ordinary Roman chamomile can be started from seed, which is much less expensive. (See box opposite).

In an area receiving light shade, plant either the tiny-leaved Corsican mint with its crème-de-menthe scent at 4in (10cm) intervals, or the pungent, peppermint–scented pennyroyal at 9in (23cm) intervals.

It is not a good idea to border your herb lawn, especially a chamomile lawn, against a grass lawn or wild–garden area, as creeping weeds will soon invade. Uprooting these weeds will disturb the herbs; chamomile is especially shallow–rooting. A surround of paving, blocks or bricks is ideal.

Herbs suitable for a herb lawn

Chamomile (Roman), chamomile 'Treneague', corn mint, Corsican mint, pennyroyal and thyme (creeping).

Herb hanging baskets

ALTHOUGH EVERY garden centre and plant market these days sells ready–planted hanging baskets, you may struggle to find one comprising herbs. And even then, as an organic gardener, you cannot guarantee that the compost in the hanging basket is ethically sourced.

So, to save time – and money – make up a herb basket yourself. You don't have to fill it with plants of different shapes and sizes, either. I have grown baskets with just one plant that look good and are incredibly useful. Suitable herbs for a hanging basket are listed on page 166.

Planting up the basket

1 Make sure your basket is stable. You can use its chains to hang it from a greenhouse support or wall bracket, but it may be easier to remove them and pop the basket on a bench, or even on the floor. If the basket has a plastic liner, make some drainage holes with scissors.

2 Begin filling your basket with a peat–free compost, adding some water–retaining granules if necessary. They are not particularly organic in their origins, but they do mean that you have to water less, which is a huge benefit in times of drought.

3 Place your plants into the basket with trailing herbs around the outer rim and taller herbs in the centre. If your basket allows you to plant through its sides, then place them through the liner and into the compost.

4 Top up with compost, and give the basket a good water to settle in the plants. Until it is ready to go out, it is best to hang it in the greenhouse, a warm, well–lit conservatory or a bright room.

Herb tubs and troughs

THESE CONTAINERS are ideal for standing on a patio, path or driveway, or next to a door. But they can also look very good when stood in borders. The tubs, raised slightly on blocks, can be placed in a part of the garden that is not at its best when the herbs in the tub are at their most attractive. A list of suitable herbs for patio tubs and troughs is given on page 165. You can also use a herb window box which is ideal for bringing extra interest to a small garden and for convenience. The process of planting – which should be carried out after the box has been put into position and secured – is similar to that used for the tub described below.

Planting up a tub

1 Place the tub or trough in its final position before you start. Put some coarse material, such as broken flowerpots or stones into the base. Do not completely block the drainage holes (if there are no holes, then you should drill some), since excess water needs to be able to escape.

2 Then fill the tub two–thirds full with a peat–free potting compost, and firm the compost as you go. If compost is allowed to dry out, the plants will not be able to suck up what they need to survive, let alone thrive. So mix water–retaining granules into the compost as you plant.

3 The best plants to put into a tub already come in pots. Remove the pots and set the plants in the tub where they are to go. As a guide, one plant in the centre and four or five around the edge of a tub 12in (30cm) across is about right.

4 Fill around the root balls with more compost and ensure that you do not leave any air pockets – this can cause the roots to dry out. Firm gently and water well.

Herbs in growing bags

GROWING BAGS are polythene bolsters of compost. They contain coir, recycled composted green products, sometimes with sand or bark added, and of course they also can contain peat. You will often find that the compost in the bags has been impregnated with fertilizers to help the plants during the first few weeks, or pesticides to ward off the major insect pests, as well as the increasingly important water–saving gel granules. As an organic gardener you should be steering clear of peat, man–made fertilizers and pesticides, so read the labels well.

Herbs in a growing bag

1 Start by placing the bag in its permanent position. For herbs, a bag should be placed outside in a sunny place. Then cut it open. Most bags have printed on them the ideal places for making the cuts, but this generally refers to the 'usual' vegetable crops of tomatoes, peppers and aubergines (typically three plants per bag), cucumbers (two), or strawberries (six to eight). For herbs such as parsley, basil, coriander and marjoram, the maximum plants to be held in a single, standard–sized growing bag are eight.

2 Loosen the compost within the bag if it appears to be compacted, and water it if it seems to be dry. Plant young herbs or sow seed thinly and evenly along the centre of the bag.

3 Cover the seeds by lightly raking the compost surface with a small fork. Then water. To test whether an established growing bag needs watering, press a piece of newspaper onto the compost. If it picks up water, the bag is moist enough. If not, a drink is needed.

Feeding in growing bags

Unlike tomatoes and peppers, herbs do not require constant feeding with special fertilizers. With normal leafy herbs, a monthly feed during the growing season with a weak liquid seaweed fertilizer will suffice.

Good for gardeners generally, and great for organic gardeners in particular, herbs are relatively easy-going plants. Most are not difficult to grow, and by their perennial nature they return year after year, or self-seed themselves so you never seem to be without them. But, like every other type of garden, a herb garden needs regular care and attention if it is to look good and give its best.

Caring for herbs

Weeding herbs

WHEN YOU are first setting out herbs in your garden, make sure that the ground is completely weed-free to give the plants the best possible start. Organic gardeners should not use proprietary weedkiller, so there isn't usually much option other than to hoe out or hand-weed as soon as you see them. Try not to let weeds seed or else the problem will become worse.

By far the easiest weeds to control are annuals, which are best kept in check by hoeing and mulching. The more troublesome weeds, however, are the perennial weeds, such as ground elder, couch grass (or twitch), bindweed, docks, thistles and perennial nettles. These will all come up year after year if left to their own devices. It is always best to remove these by hand, digging out as much of the root as possible.

One certain method of killing them, and which involves no chemicals, is to cover the area with black plastic in the spring, and leave it down until the autumn, at least. Starved of light and hence food, the weeds' leaves and roots will eventually give up. You will need time and patience for this, so it is not suitable for everyone. See also the advice on mulching on page 72.

▲ **Organic gardeners must be prepared to hand-weed – and to do it often to prevent colonies of weeds developing.**

Did you know?

Weeds with tap roots (such as dandelion and docks) should be lifted out with a garden spade or fork, and preferably when the soil is moist, so there is less risk of the root snapping while still in the ground. If it snaps and a piece is left underground it will then resprout and your energies will be doubled in trying to get rid of it.

Beware the horsetail

Horsetail (*Equisetum arvense*) is a tough, spiky weed generally regarded as the worst weed of all to eradicate. Its roots go down 2–3ft (60–90cm), and often more, making them practically impossible to completely dig out. This weed is usually associated with badly drained land, so its appearance is a warning that the area is likely to be unsuitable for growing herbs anyway.

Watering herbs

ALL PLANTS need water to survive – and grow – and it is important never to allow them to dry out completely. Whilst many herbs – such as rosemary – either need, or are tolerant of, a dry soil, there are many that perform best in full sun, but actually need a soil that is moist. Angelica, bergamot and mint fall into this latter category.

Watering a new herb garden is essential, until the plants have become established – and this could take a couple of years. Even after this length of time you should always water your plants during hot and dry spells. The best times to water are either early in the day or in the evening – when the sun is low in the sky and evaporation will be at its slowest.

With threats of climate change (and the likelihood of drier summers and more frequent droughts), it is environmentally sensible to save as much natural rainwater as possible. I have 4 water butts and a colleague has 13. If you have the space you can link the butts so that when one has filled, it overflows into the next.

Watering herbs in containers

HERBS IN patio pots, tubs, hanging baskets and window boxes will dry out more quickly than plants in the ground because they are usually placed in a sunny, exposed position.

Automatic watering systems with a timer mechanism can be installed easily. They are attached to a mains water tap, and the pipes run along the areas for watering. The water exits from these pipes either through 'seep holes', or from stand–pipes with a jet nozzle to regulate the spray and its direction of coverage.

Remember that in their dormant period, in winter, container–grown herbs (and herbs in the open soil) should be kept barely moist, or root rotting may result.

Collecting rainwater in water butts – or tanks like this – is fundamental to the organic gardening ethos.

Fatal watering

It can be a fatal mistake to water plants 'little and often'. If you merely sprinkle the surface of the soil, plant roots will be forced to stay up where the water is, in the top layer of soil. Forget to sprinkle for a few days during hot weather and there will be no reserves of water below. Therefore, a good soaking every few days is better for plants.

Mulching herbs

MULCH IS a layer of material put around plants and on top of the soil surface. It may be of organic origin (compost, manure, leaf mould or bark), or inorganic (gravel, stone or slate chippings, thick plastic or decorative glass nuggets). Putting down a mulch is a way of copying the natural state of meadows and pastures with their accumulation of dead herbs and grasses on the soil surface, or of forest floors with their fallen leaves and pine needles.

A 2in (5cm) layer of mulch spread over a warmed, moist soil in spring has several beneficial effects. Preventing evaporation is the first. Suppressing weed growth is another (if weeds do seed in the mulch they are easily pulled up). Gradually adding to the soil humus by the action of earthworms is a third benefit.

Organic mulching materials

HOMEMADE COMPOSTS and leaf mould are full of plant goodness and are certainly the easiest products to get hold of – or make yourself. Farmyard manure is also excellent, but a ready supply is not so easily sourced. As explained earlier, these materials should be applied when they are well rotted.

Use well-rotted compost or manure on poor soils and around 'hungry' herbs such as mint and chives; elsewhere use homemade leaf mould or bought-in bark products or even bagged peat-free compost.

Homemade compost
Garden and kitchen waste, mown grass clippings, shredded shrub and hedge trimmings, and so on, are converted into usable, well-rotted material for a mulch in as little as six or seven months if the conditions are right. It will hold water in the soil, and a thick layer will also provide winter protection for tender plants.

▲ **Mulching with leaf mould conditions the soil and helps to prevent weed growth and moisture loss.**

Homemade leaf mould
This is made by laying down rotted leaves collected together and compressed over several years. Although not particularly high in nutrients, it adds fibre to the soil, improves drainage, helps to retain moisture, and prevents weed seed germination. You can rarely find this to buy, however.

Farmyard manure
This is the best material if you want to feed the soil and increase its moisture-retaining capabilities; manure from pigs and horses is most commonly available, usually from farms that put up signs. Sometimes a town-based garden centre will be able to order it in for you. It is not particularly expensive to buy and produces luxuriant plant growth.

Bark
This is relatively cheap, light and biodegradable, and has excellent moisture-retaining and weed-suppressing qualities. It is available in

Bark chippings are relatively cheap, lightweight and they are biodegradable.

Glass nuggets can be used as a decorative mulch and are most at home in a contemporary garden.

'pulverised', 'shredded' and 'chipped' forms, and in several different colours. The downside to using bark is that it needs regularly topping up, and its appearance is not always to everyone's taste. It also removes nitrogen from the soil as it rots down, which is a drawback as this element is required for good plant growth.

Inorganic mulching materials

A NYTHING LOW and flat can be used as an inorganic mulch around plants: bits of old carpet, thick cardboard, plastic sheeting and specially made mulching fabrics. The trouble with these is that they are not particularly attractive. Here are just two of the more aesthetically appealing options.

Gravel, and slate or stone chippings
Many herbs are happiest when a layer of chippings or small-grade gravel is laid around them because it stops water and mud splashing

up on to the leaves. Stone mulches are long lasting and there is a huge range of colours and size grades to choose from. There are downsides to using them, however. For example, in the autumn when leaves fall it is difficult to sweep or clear the area. A thin layer of gravel will afford some moisture retention in the soil, but to do this effectively the layer should be thick – 3in (7.5cm) or more. No matter how thick a gravel mulch, weeds will always seem to germinate in it, but they are usually quite easy to remove.

Glass nuggets
This sounds dangerous, but it is safe to be around because the sharp edges have been rounded off during the manufacturing process. It has similar qualities to gravel, but is much more expensive; it does seem to blend particularly well in modern and contemporary herb gardens. It is available in a range of bright colours.

Pruning and cutting back

JUST AS different types of hedge need cutting in different ways or at different times, so herbs are variable in their clipping, pruning, cutting and tidying requirements. One extreme occurs in a formal herb garden where it is important to keep plants clipped and neat and tidy. Here, some plant types will need cutting only twice a year, but others may require more frequent light trims to keep them in shape.

In an informal garden, without the limitations of space, it is good to leave herbs to develop their characteristic shapes (such as the attractive grey–green spires of rosemary, or the rounded, voluminous globes of lavender). However, many herbs grow prolifically if left to themselves, and need frequent cutting back if the garden is not to become untidy and overgrown.

Shrubby herbs – hyssop, lavender, sage, savory and thymes, for example – should be clipped after they have flowered to remove the dead heads and maintain their natural shapes. Hyssop, particularly, has a tendency to develop bare, woody stems, so do not be afraid to prune its growths quite hard.

In late winter or spring cut out any dead pieces from shrubby herbs. If they are straggly and woody after winter, this is also the time to try cutting them back hard. Rosemary and sage both respond well to cutting at this time, however, if sage is particularly old it may be better replaced. Tall perennial herbs, such as fennel, lovage and tarragon, will almost certainly need cutting back to limit their size. The whole plant can be cut back to 12–24in (30–60cm) as fresh young shoots will grow up from the base.

With many herbs, including sage, you can cut around the outside of the clump, leaving the centre to grow up and flower: this gives a tidy look and can be most attractive; it also allows seeds to form and be collected. Note that in an

▲ **Rosemary responds well to being cut back – to maintain size and shape – in late winter or spring.**

exposed garden, if a herb is made 'artificially tall' in this way, it may need some form of staking or support. Vigorous mint plants can be treated in a similar way (but keep a look out for creeping, rooting overground stems, which should be pulled or cut off at the base of the plant). These tasks should be carried out during the summer.

Box hedges should be clipped whenever necessary during the growing season, but only until autumn – do it any later than this and the tender new growth subsequently produced could be damaged by frost.

At the very end of the season, cut down the old growth and seed heads from perennial herbs that die down in winter, including angelica, fennel, lovage, mint and tarragon.

▲ **Thyme should be clipped after it has flowered, to remove the dead heads and to maintain its natural shape.**

Using the clippings

You can often use the pruned clippings from herbs for culinary or household use, but any spares should be added to the compost heap. Spring is a good time to do some initial tidying, but many plants will need cutting back more during summer or autumn. These are all good times for adding to the compost heap, as warmer temperatures encourage speedier decomposition.

Did you know?

Many of our evergreen herbs are suitable for topiary – the art of making 'sculptures' from living plants. Bay, box, upright germander, santolina, savory and sweet myrtle can all be shaped, as can rosemary, which was a favourite during the time of Shakespeare. But remember that topiary needs regular trimming: at least two regular trims a year, plus attention to wayward or straggly shoots at other times. Late spring or early summer after new shoots have grown is ideal for one main trim; then do another in late summer, allowing time for subsequent new shoots to become 'hard' before the frosts of winter.

All plants, sadly, are susceptible to pests and diseases, and although herbs are perfect for the organic gardener because they tend to have fewer problems than most other productive plants, there are nevertheless a few problems that occur.

Organic pest and disease control

Pests of herbs

BY FAR and away the best way to prevent pests is to practise good husbandry – a lovely old gardening term, meaning to cultivate sensibly and 'hygienically'. In gardening, the word 'hygiene' is used in the context of keeping an area clean of unwanted plants, weeds, moss, algae and debris, all of which could be the breeding grounds for pests.

Organic gardeners, who choose not to use man–made chemicals, have more of a problem than other gardeners. However, a combination of being vigilant and using products approved by the various organic bodies and institutes in your country – and when only absolutely necessary – are the ways forward.

Fortunately, as we have already seen, herbs are generally less prone to attack by insect pests than other plants around the garden. This is because many of the plants contain fragrant aromatic oils that have insect repellant properties.

▼ **Growing the perfect organic herb garden is achievable, provided one is aware of the potential for pest and disease problems.**

▲ **Aphids can be found on many herbs, and although they do not kill plants directly, they do spread harmful viruses.**

Greenfly and blackfly

APHIDS, AS these insects are generically known, can be found on herbs such as angelica, anise, borage, poppies and the seed heads of dill and fennel. However, they will also attack a wide range of other plants, usually colonizing the areas of soft growth, such as the young, succulent shoot tips. These insects also spread virus diseases from plant to plant, causing a considerable amount of damage.

The aphids that attack your dill, or poppies, or garden vegetables such as broad beans, or decorative plants such as roses, may be a slightly different species of aphid, but they are not always fussy as to the type of plant they feed off, so all should be controlled as soon as they are seen.

Their feeding is unlikely to kill an established herb, but it will distort the buds and leaves, which can certainly ruin the appearance, make them unpalatable, or destroy the flowering potential of a plant for the whole season.

Aphids also excrete honeydew, which attracts an unsightly black fungus called sooty mould. Again, this looks unsightly and in severe cases will debilitate a plant, but not actually kill it.

Small infestations of aphids should be cut away and the infested parts thrown in the bin. Larger infestations may be sprayed with an organically approved pesticide. There are several insecticides and organic systemic aphicides – created from natural plant extracts – available now, and they all vary slightly in their formulations and their prices. A typical garden centre or shop will have a selection, and you should read the labels to decide on the best product for your situation. Also, aphids can be controlled, but not actually killed off, by spraying affected plants with soapy water.

Natural predators of aphids

Lacewing larvae eat aphids, as do hover fly and ladybird adults (below) and larvae. In fact, ladybirds tend to lay their eggs close to aphid colonies. Try to encourage insects such as these into the herb garden. One way to do this, for example, is to grow nasturtiums, which attract hover flies.

Biological aphid controls are available commercially in the form of *Aphidius*, a slender black insect about ⅛in (2mm) long that lays single eggs into immature aphids, killing them as the new *Aphidius* develops. A single female can lay 100 eggs in her lifetime. For this treatment to work, a temperature of 68°F (18°C) is required for at least two hours a day, so there are only certain times of the year – in most temperate countries – where this will work effectively.

⚠ **Snails eat the soft, fleshy leaves of many herbs, and they have a particular liking for the tops of seedlings.**

Slugs and snails

FOR MANY gardeners, these are the number one pest. They like damp but not sodden positions, and their favourite foods are the soft, fleshy leaves and stems of seedlings. In the herb garden they tend to ignore the silver or felt-leaved species, but young shoots of soft-leaved herbs are particularly attractive to them.

Organic gardeners should avoid baits (based on metaldehyde or methiocarb), but there are clay-based baits that are similar. They have mixed results in terms of effectiveness though. I have tried the old wives' tales of putting down half a grapefruit or melon (which attracts slugs in numbers where they can be collected and disposed of), and also beer traps, where they are lured into a slop-trough of beer. Keep the container about 1in (2.5cm) above ground level, as this reduces the number of beneficial insects that may crawl in and drown.

A few years ago I tried the biological controls – nematodes that you water onto the soil around susceptible plants. This was – probably – the most successful form of control I've come across. The reason for my caution, however, is that controlling slugs and snails 'biologically' in this way is expensive, and you're never quite sure of the success rate as you don't see the slug carnage that you see when pellets are used!

And talking of pellets, there are some pellets that have approval for use from the usual organic authorities. These pellets are usually clay-based and, whereas they do not contain poisons to kill the slugs, the clay within the pellets is supposed to cause the slugs to dehydrate. In my experience the slug soon realizes that it is dehydrating so quickly moves on, therefore the pellets are not entirely satisfactory.

Copper bands and rings, set around plants, or around the rims of containers, have proved successful. The mollusc gets a mild electric shock as it slides up to and touches the copper, so it makes a retreat and leaves the plant, or plants, alone. This is a successful control, and it is humane, but it is expensive and it does not put paid to the existence of the pest, which merely moves on to some other, less protected plant.

Red spider mites

THESE ARE very persistent pests that flourish in hot, dry conditions, such as those found in a greenhouse or the home. Eggs overwinter – on plants as well as in cracks in the greenhouse or even cracks indoors – and hatch in the spring. The adult pests feed on the plant's sap, and attacks are evident by a pale stippling of its leaves accompanied by fine webbing around the plant. Succulent-leaved herbs that are grown under

Eggshell barriers

Plants particularly vulnerable to slugs can be surrounded by crushed eggshells or grit. The slugs dislike sliding across these, so usually go elsewhere.

▲ Red spider mites are more likely to attack plants under glass or in the home, but in dry, warm summers they also attack outdoor plants.

▲ A number of different caterpillar species attack herbs; if there are not too many, pick them off by hand.

glass – or even indoors – are particularly vulnerable. *Aloe vera* and basil are two herbs I have found to be particularly vulnerable.

Control the pests by keeping up humidity levels around plants (such as by standing the pots on trays of regularly dampened gravel), or by introducing the predatory *Phytoseiulus*, a tiny mite that feeds on the pests. However, there needs to be a minimum night temperature of 63°F (16°C) and day temperatures in the 70–85°F (20–30°C) range for this control to work.

Caterpillars

THERE ARE a number of different caterpillars – the larval stages of moths and butterflies – that will devour the foliage and flowers of a wide range of herbs. If they are not too numerous, pick them off by hand. Otherwise, spray with a suitable, organically approved insecticide.

Steinernema carpcapse is a commercially available nematode for the biological control of caterpillars. Three applications stored in the fridge, and used at five to seven day intervals will ensure that all hatchlings and generations of a given caterpillar species are killed. The control should be applied when the caterpillars are first seen. You will need to mix the nematodes into a spray solution and apply this directly to the caterpillars – pests not directly sprayed will not be controlled.

▷ These carrots have been attacked by the carrot fly pest, which can also attack parsley and other herbs in the umbellifer family.

Carrot fly

IN EARLY summer, the grub of the carrot fly tunnels into the roots of plants. Its main target is, of course, the carrot, but it will also attack roots of other plants in the same family, particularly parsley. It causes the foliage to become discoloured, and the plant could eventually die. The older leaves start to turn yellow and droop, and they become tinged with red. Pull up and destroy any affected plants to get rid of the pests.

A preventative option is to put a polythene barrier 2½ft (75cm) high around susceptible plants during mid–spring. Or you could cover up plants with horticultural fleece while the plants are young. Growing carrots, obviously, attracts the pest in the first instance, but sowings made after mid–summer miss the first generation of carrot fly. And it is a good idea to raise two batches of parsley each year, so that you have a replacement supply to plant on a different site.

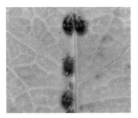

▲ **Leaf miners (left) attack a range of plants, whilst scale insects (right) target woody plants such as bay and citrus.**

▲ **The vine weevil (left) damages plant roots, whilst rosemary beetles (right) eat the leaves of some herbs.**

Leaf miners

GENERALLY, LEAF miners attack a range of garden plants as well as some vegetables. Yellowish or yellowish-purple blotches occur on the upper surface of the older leaves, usually near the centre. Any kind of insecticide is fairly ineffective as the spray runs off the foliage. On small plants you can remove mined leaves but not if this would result in significant defoliation.

Rosemary beetles

THESE ARE a minor pest. Small, shiny, dark green beetles, they are distinguished by purple strips on their wing cases. They eat the leaves and tips of lavender, rosemary, sage and thyme. Hand–pick and destroy the beetles and larvae.

Scale insects

THESE LOOK like waxy, brownish, flattish, oval lumps, seemingly immobile, gathered on the backs of leaves or on the stems of bay and citrus trees. Leaves also become covered with sticky, black, sooty mould. Rub off the scales gently before the infestation builds up, or spray with a liquid horticultural soap (organically approved).

Vine weevils

THESE ARE an important pest, affecting plants in the ground or in pots. In spring and early autumn you will see horrid white grubs with orange heads. Repot plants and destroy any grubs you see, or water plants with nematodes (eelworms) in autumn. The worms destroy the vine weevil grubs, however, the soil temperature must be above 40°F (5°C) for this to work.

Suckers

BAY (IN the spring) and box (throughout the summer) can be attacked by sucker insects. The leaf margins of bay are thickened, curled and turn yellow, while box leaves become stunted. Cut out and burn affected shoots.

Cuckoo spit

THIS IS not really a serious problem for your plants. The 'spit' is caused by the grub of the sap–sucking froghopper insect. Lavender, rosemary, southernwood and roses are the most frequently infested plants. Pick off the pests by hand and destroy them.

◄ **Cuckoo spit is the unsightly frothy mass that the sap-sucking froghopper insect surrounds itself with for protection.**

Diseases of herbs

AS WITH pests, being vigilant and good hygiene are very important for preventing diseases. Bacterial and fungal diseases do occasionally strike, but as mentioned before herbs are not particularly prone to too many problems.

Mildew

THERE ARE two different types of mildew – powdery mildew and downy mildew. Powdery mildew is more common for herbs and covers young leaves, buds and stems with its white mycelium. Older parts of plants are generally resistant to mildew. Cool, wet weather makes ideal conditions for the spores (which are carried on the wind) to germinate. They most readily infest plants that are slightly dehydrated, or if there is poor air circulation in the vicinity of the plant. Downy mildew is characterized by greyish–brown pustules on the undersides of the leaves. For both mildews the recommendations for organic control are the same:

• remove infected leaves promptly
• improve air circulation around plants by increased spacing and good weed control – if under cover, improve ventilation
• keep plants adequately watered but avoid overhead watering.

▼ **Mildew appears as a white, powder-like covering over leaves, stems and sometimes flowers.**

Rust

MINT, PYRETHRUM and comfrey are particularly susceptible to the fungal disease rust. It is an aptly named disease, for the telltale signs are bright orange, rust–like pustules that appear on both sides of the leaves before spreading to other parts of the plant. It is most rampant in damp, cool weather. The disease is hard to eradicate because it overwinters as spores on the soil, as well as on fallen leaves.

Botrytis

THIS IS a fungus that attacks many plants, especially if grown under glass, including basil, pelargoniums, tomatoes, strawberries, roses and sunflowers. Seen as a grey mould (which is an often–used common name for the problem), it thrives in high humidity. Control is difficult because the fungus is so widespread. Remove all dead and injured parts of plants before they have a chance to become infected. Remove infected parts promptly and cut right back into healthy wood.

▼ **Rust is a fungal disease that attacks many plants (left). Botrytis fungus on pelargonium leaves (right).**

Harvesting herbs is a continuous process, and, once they are established, most herbs will grow strongly enough to allow plenty of repeat harvesting. You can then select a number of methods to preserve them before turning them into dried culinary herbs, oils, vinegars and tinctures.

Harvesting, drying and preserving herbs

Harvesting herbs

CUTTING PERENNIAL, shrubby herbs has a dual purpose in that you can make use of the cut pieces, and you are effectively pruning the plants as well; aim to improve their overall shape as you harvest from them. However, it makes sense not to strip small, immature herbs of all their leaves and/or flowers, since this will seriously shorten their lives. Many annuals, such as lovage will, however, produce a second crop once they have flowered, if they are cut back almost to the ground.

The optimum time for collecting herb material to preserve it for later use will usually be during the growing season. A few herbs (including rosemary, sage and thyme) may also be lightly picked when dormant, but they will not have such a strong flavour.

▼ **When harvesting herbs, pick only healthy material: avoid any that is dead, damaged, diseased or discoloured.**

▲ **Don't harvest too many herbs at one time; heaps of herbs waiting to be processed will start to deteriorate.**

Picking in perfect condition

Leaves Pick stems of small–leaved plants for stripping later; larger leaves may be picked individually. Pick them before the plants have come into flower as leaf flavour and texture will be at its best.

Flowers Pick single blooms or flower heads as appropriate, and strip off petals or florets when spreading them to dry. These should be cut soon after they have opened, when they are at their best, and not left to drop their petals, when colour, scent and flavour will be seriously reduced.

Rules for harvesting fresh herbs

- Choose a still, sunny day for picking, so that the essential oil content, which gives the plant its flavour and scent, is in optimum condition.

- Wait until any dew or rainfall has evaporated since herbs can go mouldy before the drying process is complete if picked when wet.

- Aim to finish harvesting herbs in the morning before volatile oils within the cells of the plants have been drawn to the surface by the heat and dissipated.

- Pick only healthy material from plants – avoid the five 'd's: stems that are dead, deteriorating, damaged, diseased or discoloured.

- Use only sharp and clean secateurs (for thicker or woody stems) or scissors (for thinner or fleshier stems); they need to be sharp so as not to damage the plant and limit further cropping. Make sure that sticky blades do not pass diseases from plant to plant.

- Harvest only as much as you can deal with at one time. Herbs should not be left in heaps, waiting to be processed, as even quite a small pile waiting for a short period can start to deteriorate.

- Before processing the material (leaves and flowers), wipe it so that it is clean and insect-free. Lightly use a sponge and pat dry with a paper towel afterwards; do not wash it as this will impede drying.

Roots Generally these are harvested when the plant is in its dormant period (late autumn or winter). When lifting, leave enough root attached to the plant so that it can continue growing. It is important to wash the roots thoroughly with cold tap water, to dry them and then to cut them into pieces of convenient size before processing.

Seeds Seed heads, or pods, must be picked as soon as they are ripe – this is usually the period after they have stopped being green and before they fall from the plant. Keep an eye on them for some plants ripen and disperse their seeds relatively quickly.

▷ **Seed heads are best harvested when they are ripe – after they have stopped being green but before they fall from the plant.**

Drying herbs

THE AIM when drying herbs is to remove the moisture in the fresh material without sacrificing the volatile oil content. Try to complete the process quickly, as a slow drying process will mean that oils are lost through decay and deterioration. However, quick drying by providing excessive heat will also cause the oils to be lost. The key is to provide the right temperature with low humidity.

Commercial growers dry herbs in large kilns set at around 99°F (38°C). This is difficult to replicate at home and not really sustainable as it uses up too much energy. However, the temperatures you would find in an airing cupboard, which are in the 68–90°F (20–32°C) range, should be sufficient.

Also, keep the material out of the direct line of the sun. Sun drying is a traditional method in climates where air temperatures are high and humidity low, but it does lead to colour loss.

Oven drying is generally too fierce for flowers and foliage, even at its lowest setting, but it is suitable for roots.

Drying leaves

THE OLD traditional way to dry leaves was to tie herbs in bunches with raffia or string, and hang them up in a clean, airy place. If you

▲ Hang stems, branches or sprigs of herbs, tied into bunches with string or raffia, in a warm, dry, airy place.

don't have a suitable place, you can spread leaves either on slatted trays or on fine netting stretched over a frame so that air can circulate beneath. They should then be stored in a warm, dark, well-ventilated place, and left there until they are

▼ Wait until any dew or rainfall has evaporated before harvesting herbs, as they can rapidly go mouldy if too wet.

◁ **Once bunches of lavender flowers are dried, they can be stripped, and the individual blooms stored in airtight jars.**

Specially treated silica gel or dry sand can also be used for drying flowers, resulting in a perfect shape and a good colour. Take a container such as a plastic sandwich box and place a ½in (1cm) or so layer of the silica or sand in the bottom. Then lay your chosen flower on it, and sift more sand gently over the flower until it is covered. Try to get the sand in amongst the petals without dislodging or squashing them. Leave the box for about three weeks in a warm, dry place.

Saving and drying seeds

THE BEST way to dry seeds is to pick the seed heads with the stems still attached. Tie them into bunches and insert the heads into paper bags. As with drying lavender (see above), these should then be hung in a warm, airy place. When dry, carefully empty the bags on to a clean surface, and strip the seeds of their husks or pods, before storing in labelled envelopes. Seeds should not be stored in plastic bags, which can hold moisture.

crackly–dry, which would normally take three or four weeks. When dry, strip the leaves off the stems (where relevant), or crumble larger ones into smaller pieces ready to store.

Drying flowers

FLOWERS ARE much more delicate than leaves. Carefully twist off the heads of large blooms (such as roses), and spread out the petals on paper or slatted trays. Put them in a warm place and leave them until they are papery dry.

It is easier to dry some flower heads whole (such as those of pot marigold); when they are dry the head can, if required, be twisted off for the petals to be stored or used individually. Lavender is best hung up in bunches, in the old–fashioned way, tied loosely with string or raffia, and with the heads inside paper bags. Once the lavender flowers are dry, they can be left whole (for use in pillows or pot–pourri), or stripped from the stems in the same way as small leaves (see above).

Rosebuds or chive flowers for decoration will keep good shape if they are dried upright, with the stems pushed through florist's oasis.

How to dry roots

Scrub the roots clean, then cut them in pieces and spread them over a baking tray. To dry properly, roots require a temperature in the 120°–140°F (50°–60°C) range. Use an oven, at a very low setting, with the door left open. Turn them at intervals to ensure that they receive an even heat. Leave them there until they are brittle, but do test this often. The length of time they need in the oven depends on the root sizes and moisture content.

Other preserving methods

Drying herbs in the microwave

Microwaves are an excellent way to dry small amounts of herbs without affecting the flavour – and speedily, too. Place a sheet of kitchen towel on the base plate in the microwave, and then lay either individual leaves of the herb you are drying, or a couple of small bunches on top. Try to make sure that the leaves or bunches are not touching. Turn the microwave power setting to 'low', and turn it on for two minutes. Check after about a minute that all is going well and that the leaves have not already turned to a crisp. Turn the power back on, and check again after half a minute or so. The aim is to get the leaves to be crisp and papery. The eventual timing will depend on the sizes of the leaves and the amount of moisture within them.

▶ **Place the dried herbs into small dishes to cool and to keep drying, before storing them in airtight containers.**

▼ **It is more convenient to microwave-dry short stems of rosemary than to strip off individual leaves.**

▼ **These purple sage leaves have dried perfectly in just 2½ minutes in a microwave oven set on low power.**

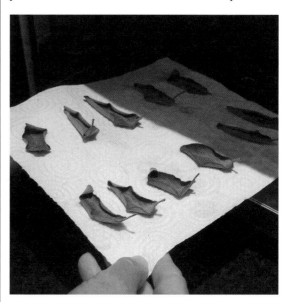

△ **To store herbs in ice cubes, finely chop the leaves, then drop some into ice-cube tray compartments.**

▷ **Top up each compartment with cold water, and immediately place the tray in the freezer.**

Preserving herbs by freezing

ONE OF the best ways to keep the flavour of herbs is to freeze them in ice cubes for adding to soups, stews and other cooked dishes (e.g. chervil and Sweet Cicely) or for use in drinks (e.g. mint and borage). Chop the herb leaves finely. Drop some into compartments in an ice–cube tray, and top up with water. Place in the freezer.

A good way of preserving herbs that do not keep a good aroma when dried (such as basil, parsley, chives and mint) is to freeze whole sprigs. In fact most herbs used in cooking, if stripped from the stems but not chopped, can be frozen in plastic bags. They should remain in good condition for three or four months.

△ **Herb ice cubes can be available the same day, if frozen in the early morning.**

▽ **Ice cubes containing chopped mint and borage are great for summer drinks, whilst chervil, Sweet Cicely and salad burnet can be used in soups, stews and other cooked dishes.**

Preserving herbs in sugar

SUGAR MAKES an excellent preservative for some herbs. Flower sugars are fun: pound the flowers of jasmine, rosemary, rose petals and violets together with three times their own weight of caster sugar. Then store in an airtight jar in a dark place.

Lavender sugar, also, is a great way to instil the delicate fragrance of lavender in cakes, meringues and biscuits. Bruise dried lavender flowers, stripped from the stem, and add them to caster sugar or icing sugar before storing in an airtight jar. Leave for at least two weeks, and upon use sieve out the flowers. Ten to fifteen heads of lavender should be sufficient to lend fragrance to 1lb (450g) of sugar.

Herb oils, vinegars and tinctures

Preserving herbs in vegetable oils or in vinegar is an easy and rewarding thing to try yourself at home. A mixed–herb oil, or one with a single flavour (such as basil or marjoram) can add interest to pizza and pasta dishes, stir-fries, salad dressings, and grilled or barbecued meat, fish or even vegetables.

Herb vinegars are similar, often adding a sharpness to sweet dishes. Some can also be used as antiseptics for cleaning, and medicinally some can be used as poultices, or dabbed on the skin to counteract various conditions, or even to be taken internally as a tonic.

A tincture is a solution that has been extracted from plant material after macerating in neat or diluted alcohol. Tinctures are used medicinally, and they are potent things; take

▲ **Basil oil, with its aromatic flavour, is one of the most commonly used herbal oils, especially in Italian cuisine.**

them in doses of drops or teaspoons and, I suggest, only as directed by a qualified medical practitioner.

Rosemary and garlic oils

As well as being useful in the kitchen for basting lamb and other meats, rosemary oil is the ideal ingredient for bath lotions and beauty treatments. And oil infused with garlic makes an effective liniment for relieving aches and pains.

◄ **Rosemary oil is useful for bath lotions and beauty treatments – as well as for basting lamb in the oven.**

Sweet and spicy oils

Sweet herb oils flavoured with flowers such as lavender, pinks, rose, scented pelargoniums and lemon verbena go particularly well with puddings, fruit dishes and marinades. Spicy oils are best in salad dressings and stir-fries. Use a sunflower oil and make it spicy by adding crushed seeds of coriander, dill and fennel.

Choosing the base oil

Use a good-quality, mild-flavoured oil (such as sunflower oil). Beware of strong-flavoured oils (such as extra-virgin olive oil), so that the taste does not compete with the herbs. When covering the herbs with oil, make sure that all of the herb material is submerged, as any parts left above the surface will deteriorate, and possibly taint the oil.

Making a herb oil

IT IS not difficult to make a herb oil. You will need a clean glass jar large enough to take ¾pt (400ml) of oil, and with a screw top. Put a good handful of leaves or flower heads into the jar – either a mixture (such as oregano, rosemary and thyme) or a single herb (such as marjoram) – and crush them lightly to release the essential oils.

Pour in the vegetable oil until the herbs or flowers are completely immersed. Cover the jar and stand it in a warm place – a sunny windowsill is ideal. After about a week, strain off the herbs, then replace with fresh ones in exactly the same way, and then leave to infuse for another week. This can be repeated as many times as you wish, until the oil has reached the strength of flavour you would like.

Finally, remove the herbs and pour the oil into a clean, sterilized bottle with an airtight lid. Some people like to pop in a final sprig or a few leaves before sealing the bottle but this means that it should be used up sooner. The oil should keep for a few weeks with the extra sprig, or six months or more without.

Herbs most commonly used in oils

Savoury
Basil, garlic, fennel, marjoram, mint, rosemary, tarragon, thyme and savory.

Sweet
Clove pinks, lavender, lemon verbena, rose petals and scented perlargonium.

Fennel

Lemon verbena

◁ **Cider vinegar is often used as the base for herb vinegars, as it better complements most herbs than malt, balsamic or white vinegars.**

sweet dishes and are useful as home remedies. Raspberry vinegar can help to ease a sore throat, and lavender, applied as a compress, may help relieve a headache.

To make your herb vinegar, fill a clean jar to about one-third with herb leaves, and other flavourings of your choosing, then top up with cider vinegar. Make sure all of the herbs are submerged, and leave the mixture to infuse for two or three weeks. You can also leave a sprig of herb in the solution for decorative effect.

Making a herb tincture

Herbal tinctures are best made as a cold infusion using dried herbs and alcohol with a little flavour of its own. The alcohol should be at least 60° proof (such as brandy or vodka). Surgical spirit is suitable only if the tincture is for external use.

Put the herbs in a jar and top up with a mixture of one part of water to two parts of the alcohol. As a general guide you need ½oz (15g) of dried herbs per ½pt (300ml) of alcohol/water mixture. Seal the jar and leave it in a warm, dark place for about a week. By then the active constituents will have been extracted and the herbs will start to deteriorate, so strain these out of the mixture, and rebottle.

The dosage is usually in the region of 5–15 drops, which can be taken directly, or added to a cup of hot water. It is advisable, however, to seek expert medical advice before taking any form of herbal tincture.

Making a herb vinegar

This is made in much the same way as a herb oil. A great variety of flavouring materials can be used: fresh or dried leaves, spices, chillis, garlic, fruit or flower petals.

Cider vinegar is often used as a base vinegar. You can make a refreshing toner for your face by infusing some with rose petals, or a mint-and-marigold combination, and then adding a couple of teaspoonfuls to a basin of water. Tarragon vinegar is a classic for salad dressing. Fruit and flower vinegars such as raspberry, blackberry, lavender or rose petal can add sharpness to

Herbs most commonly used in vinegars

Leaves
Basil, bay, chervil, dill, fennel, garlic, lemon balm, marjoram, mint, rosemary, savory, tarragon and thyme.

Flowers
Carnation, clover, elderflower, lavender, nasturtium, primrose, rose petal, rosemary, thyme and sweet violet.

Essential oils

THE ESSENTIAL (or volatile) oil in a herb gives it its scent. Some plants, such as lemon balm, mainly contain their essential oils in the leaves, others (including roses) mainly in their flowers.

These oils are widely used in the food, pharmaceutical and cosmetic industries. In the home they are used in aromatherapy and herbal medicine, and are taken in one or more of the following ways:
- by inhaling them in vaporizers and in fragranced products such as pot–pourri
- by massaging them into the skin
- by applying them in compresses
- by putting them in the bath
- as food flavouring (but only in very small quantities, the whole herb plant being safer and usually more satisfactory in the kitchen).

Essential oils are concentrated substances and should be taken internally only in controlled, drop–sized doses. When applied externally they must be diluted with a carrier oil. If you are pregnant, or you suffer from a chronic illness, do not expose yourself to these concentrates without first taking medical advice.

The extraction of oils is a highly complex and, needless to say, expensive business. It is not something the amateur can do at home, as complicated equipment and a huge volume of plant stock are required. For example, it takes about 250lb (115kg) of rose petals to produce 1fl oz (25ml) of essential oil. This is why your only realistic option is to buy oils from a supplier.

Bath oils

INCORPORATING DROPS of essential oil into bath water is a good way to benefit from the fragrance. Sprinkle the oil on hand–hot water after it has settled, and then swish it around gently. Do not add oils to running hot water or they will evaporate.

⚠ **Essential oils have many uses but should always be treated with caution.**

To make a bath oil for dry skins, add about 20 drops of essential oil to a small bottle containing about 2tsp (10ml) of almond or sunflower oil. If either of these latter oils have been previously infused with fresh herbs or flowers – such as chamomile or lavender – the fragrance is even better. A lavender bath, particularly, is soothing if you have a cold or are otherwise under the weather, and it is deeply relaxing, too. It is also mildly antiseptic and helps to heal small swellings, as well as tiny bites, scratches and cuts.

Inhaling essential oils

It is immensely therapeutic to breathe in the fragrance of essential oils; it can have an immediate effect on mood. The easiest way to do this is to put a few drops of oil onto a handkerchief to tuck under a pillow, or to mix some into a pot-pourri of flowers and herbs. An essential oil burner or vaporizer is more efficient, if you have one.

The next four pages, which list the jobs that need doing throughout the year, should be thought of as a general guide. The gardening year is divided into 12; by all means think of these divisions as 'months', but depending on where you live, April may be considerably warmer for you than for another reader. It is far more sensible to refer to the 12 divisions seasonally. Adjust what you do according to your first and last frost dates. If you live in an area without frost, just remember that you will need to water your herbs more!

Calendar of work

Jobs for spring

Early spring

Take root cuttings of bergamot, chamomile, hyssop, mint, tansy, sweet woodruff, Sweet Cicely, tarragon.

Sow seeds (under heat) of basil, borage, fennel, coriander, sweet marjoram, rue.

Sow seeds (in an unheated greenhouse) of chervil, chives, dill, lemon balm, lovage, parsley, sage, summer savory, sorrel.

Sow seeds (outdoors) of anise, borage, caraway, chamomile, chervil, chives, fennel, Good King Henry, parsley (cover with cloches), tansy.

Mid-spring

Plant out new hardy herbs (and tender herbs only if frost is past) as required.

Lift and divide chives, lady's mantle, lovage, marjoram, mint, pennyroyal, rue, salad burnet, sorrel, tarragon, thyme, winter savory, wormwood.

Containers can be taken out of their winter/protective quarters; watch out for watering and feeding from now on.

Prick out seedlings from early spring sowings.

Weed the herb garden.

Late spring

Take softwood cuttings of cotton lavender, curry plant, lavender, marjoram, mint, rosemary, rue, sage, southernwood, tarragon (French), winter savory, thyme.

Prune and shape bay, cotton lavender, hyssop, lavender, rue, southernwood, thyme, winter savory.

Pot on and/or harden off young plants from early spring sowings.

Harvest fresh herbs

Throughout spring, pick angelica, lemon balm, bay, borage, caraway, chervil, chives, fennel, hyssop, lovage, pot marjoram, mint, parsley, pennyroyal, peppermint, rosemary, rue, sage, winter savory, sorrel, tarragon, lemon thyme.

Jobs for summer

Early summer

Sow seeds (outdoors) of basil, borage, chervil, chives, coriander, dill, fennel, lovage, sweet marjoram, summer and winter savory.
Plant up patio containers with annual or tender herbs.
Plant out basil.
Weed the herb garden.
Layer branches of rosemary.
Water and feed outdoor herb containers and pots.
Harvest and dry sage.
Cut second-year shoots of angelica for candying.
Trim cotton lavender hedges (if flowers are not required) to maintain their shape. Trim box hedges and topiary as required.

Mid-summer

Sow seeds (outdoors) of coriander, parsley.
Take semi-ripe cuttings of bay, cotton lavender, curry plant, lavender, lemon balm, mint, myrtle, scented pelargonium, rosemary, sage, tarragon (French), winter savory, thyme, wormwood.
Water and feed outdoor herb containers and pots; if you are going away for a summer holiday, make sure you have a contingency plan so that the herb garden, or container plants, do not suffer with dryness.

Cut back lavender after flowering to maintain its shape.
Harvest and dry lemon balm, lavender, summer savory, hyssop, tarragon, rosemary, thyme.
Harvest seed of angelica, anise, caraway.

Late summer

Water outdoor herb containers and pots; see mid-summer if going away. Mint, parsley and comfrey are herbs most at risk of drying out.
Feed with a foliar feed of liquid seaweed any herbs (in the garden or in containers) that have been suffering from a pest attack.
Prune and shape bay, box, cotton lavender and curry plants to help maintain shape.
Weed the herb garden.
Harvest and dry clary sage, lavender, marjoram, sage, thyme.
Harvest and freeze mint, pennyroyal.

Harvest fresh herbs

All herbs can be gathered in during summer.

Jobs for autumn

Early autumn

Take semi-ripe cuttings of bay, box, cotton lavender, curry plant, elder, hyssop, lavender, mint, rosemary, sage, southernwood, tarragon, winter savory, thyme.

Lift and divide bergamot.

Move tender herbs such as basil and coriander into a greenhouse, or onto a kitchen windowsill, in order to keep picking.

Move containers of tender herbs (such as bay, myrtle and scented pelargonium) under cover for winter protection.

Prune and shape, for the final time of the year, bay, box, cotton lavender, curry plant and lavender to maintain shape. Do this much later and there will be a risk that autumn frost will damage any new resultant growth.

Protect tender herbs that need to remain outside (such as bay and lemon verbena).

Harvest seed of angelica, anise, caraway, chervil, fennel.

Mid-autumn

Plant out new hardy herbs.
Sow parsley seeds (under heat).
Sow seeds (outdoors) of angelica, catmint, chamomile, chervil, fennel, wormwood.

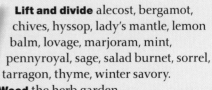

Lift and divide alecost, bergamot, chives, hyssop, lady's mantle, lemon balm, lovage, marjoram, mint, pennyroyal, sage, salad burnet, sorrel, tarragon, thyme, winter savory.

Weed the herb garden.

Top-dress any herbs that die back in autumn (including bergamot).

Harvest and dry or freeze clary sage, dandelion roots, marigold, lavender, parsley, peppermint.

Late autumn

Cut down old growth of hardy perennial herbs and collect any remaining seed heads.

Dig up and discard annual herbs (such as borage, basil, chervil, dill, coriander, summer savory and sweet marjoram), and the second–year biennials (which could include chervil, parsley and rocket).

Weed around the herbs.

Apply a mulch of leaf mould around hardy perennial and shrubby herbs.

Protect with a cloche any outdoor herbs to be used fresh over winter (such as chervil, lemon thyme, parsley and salad burnet).

Dig up and start to force chives, French tarragon and mint.

Harvest fresh herbs

Throughout autumn, pick lemon balm, basil, bay, borage, caraway, chervil, chives, clary sage, fennel, hyssop, pot marigold, pot marjoram, mint, parsley, pennyroyal, peppermint, rosemary, rue, sage, winter savory, sorrel, thyme.

Jobs for winter

Early winter

Take root cuttings of mint, pennyroyal, tansy, tarragon.
Insulate a greenhouse or conservatory where tender herbs may be overwintered.
Dig heavy (clay) soils.
Check the pH of soils every three or four years, and rectify by applying corrective compounds as required. A good way to reduce the pH in a soil that is too alkaline is to incorporate more well-rotted organic matter (such as garden compost or manure); quantities at the rate of 17lb per sq yd (9.25kg per m²) of garden compost, or 5½ lb (3kg per m²) of manure, are both sufficient to reduce the pH level by one point.
Prune elder.
Wrap terracotta or stone pots and ornaments in case they are damaged by heavy winter frosts.

Remove any dead growth from perennial herbs, to prevent pest and disease carry-over, and to prevent neighbouring non-herb plants from being smothered by dead foliage.
Remove weeds as required.
Plan changes or additions to the herb garden, such as the construction of new paths, steps, arches, fencing, walling and so on.
Order seeds needed for spring sowing.

Late winter

Clean out the greenhouse and any coldframes, giving them a good scrub with an outdoor disinfectant, to rid them of lurking pests and diseases.
Clean pots and trays similarly.
Sow seeds (under heat) of basil, borage, dill, parsley.
Sow seeds (outdoors) of chervil, cowslip, parsley, sweet cicely and sweet woodruff (allowing for a period of stratification, when the seed is necessarily exposed for a short period to cold or even freezing temperatures).

Harvest fresh herbs

Throughout winter pick bay, chervil, hyssop, lemon thyme, marjoram, parsley, rosemary, rue, sage, winter savory, winter tarragon, thyme. Basil can be harvested if grown under protection; chives, French tarragon and mint can be harvested if forced.

Mid-winter

Keep horticultural fleece handy in case of cold snaps and the need to cover herbs (seedlings, cuttings or tender plants).
Provide shelter or cover for bay trees if the temperature plummets.

This part of the book will be an invaluable source of reference when you are choosing plants to grow in your herb garden, or identifying plants you see and like. You'll be able to find the descriptions of many of our most popular garden herbs, and see what they look like, too.

Directory of herbs

Hardiness zones

BEFORE INVESTING time, effort and, of course, money on new purchases for your herb garden, you must first understand your geographical location and what this means to the plants in your care. It is particularly important to understand temperatures and the cold-tolerance of plants. For many years the standard used in America has been the Harvard University-derived 'hardiness zones'. The original zone map was of the US, but it has also been adapted for use in the UK and Europe. These maps enable gardeners to judge how plants will grow and thrive, wherever they live. Certain plants – such as garlic and the silver-leaved herbs from the Mediterranean regions, or the succulents of Mexico and South America – are obvious plant choices if you live in these zones.

If you live in the UK, or anywhere else in Europe or North America, these maps really help you to understand which plants will survive in your garden without help, or whether you need to cosset them.

Areas within the maps are colour-coded into 11 distinct zones. Plants mentioned in this part of the book will be given a zone reference from Z1 to Z11. Find your location on the maps, and you can then identify which zone your garden falls into.

Do not forget to take into account that cities are warmer than rural locations, and that putting up walls or hedges can dramatically improve conditions for plants.

KEY

- Zone 1: below -50°F (-46°C)
- Zone 2: -50 to -40°F (-46 to -40°C)
- Zone 3: -40 to -30°F (-40 to -34.5°C)
- Zone 4: -30 to -20°F (-34 to -29°C)
- Zone 5: -20 to -10°F (-29 to -23°C)
- Zone 6: -10 to 0°F (-23 to -18°C)
- Zone 7: 0 to 10°F (-18 to -12°C)
- Zone 8: 10 to 20°F (-12 to -7°C)
- Zone 9: 20 to 30°F (-7 to -1°C)
- Zone 10: 30 to 40°F (-1 to 4°C)
- Zone 11: above 40°F (above 4°C)

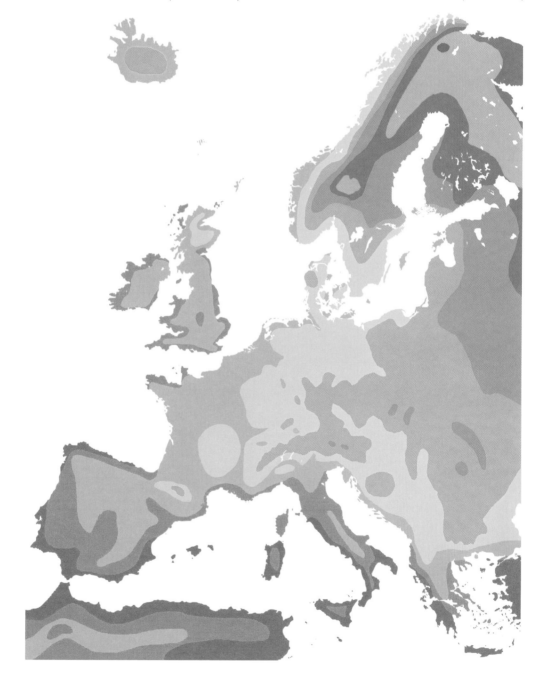

How to use this directory

Plants are listed alphabetically by their botanical or Latin names, and under each are these items of information:

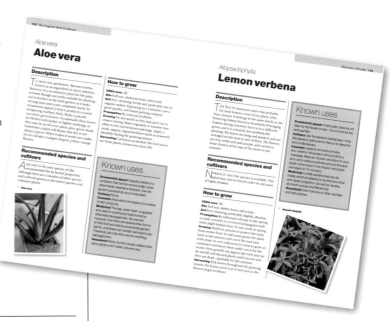

Description

Here you will discover generalized details of the plant's shape, size and general demeanour, along with flower and foliage colour and shape.

Recommended varieties

Sometimes a plant species will exist without offspring or siblings. This will therefore have a relatively small entry in this book. But with, for example, the *Lavandula* genus, there are hundreds of species, varieties and cultivars (meaning 'cultivated variety' – see below), and so there will be many to recommend.

How to grow

USDA zone – These are the climate zones referred to on pages 104–105, designed to identify the relative hardiness of plants. The zone numbers quoted here, based on UK Royal Horticultural Society data, are on the cautious side, so if you are not prepared to take any chances, follow the hardiness ratings to the letter. Otherwise there is a great deal of leeway. Raised beds, good drainage, tree cover, east–facing as opposed to west–facing gardens, and planting against a house wall all give plants a better habitat – so experiment if you want.

Site – Whether the herb in question prefers sun or shade.

Soil – The preferred type of soil.

Propagation – When to increase stock of the herb in question, and by which method(s).

Growing – Essential tips on making the best of the herb you are growing.

Harvesting – When to harvest the herb in question, and which parts of it.

Known uses

Ornamental appeal – Where the herb is seen for best effect.

Culinary – How to use parts of the herb in the kitchen.

Cosmetic – Which herb, and which parts of it, can be used for cosmetic purposes.

Medicinal – Which herb, and which parts of it, can be used medicinally.

Household – Which herb to use around the home, and for what purpose.

How plants are named

IF THE name of the plant is all in italics, then this is a naturally occurring plant that has been discovered growing in its wild habitat, and then been grown in number to be introduced to gardens. Take *Lavandula stoechas* for example. *Lavandula* is the genus name and *stoechas* is the species name; this is a plant that was originally discovered growing wild in areas from Spain to Greece, and therefore it is a 'true' species.

Different plant hunters and botanists have, over the years, found slightly different forms or variations of recognized species, so sometimes you will see f. or var. or subsp. in the names of the plants. These describe naturally occurring forms (f.), varieties (var.) or subspecies (subsp.). An example of this is the plant *Lavandula stoechas* subsp. *stoechas* f. *leucantha*.

However, if you see a name such as *Lavandula stoechas* 'Anouk', this tells you that the plant is a cultivar. Plant breeders and hybridizers select and cross plants to produce and reproduce a distinctive plant that they can then name. Therefore, if you see a plant name that has part of it within quote marks, as above, you will know that this is a cultivar (contraction of cultivated variety) and not a true species.

A hybrid is a cross between two species, or genera, and it is indicated by a cross in the name (eg. *Lavandula* x *intermedia*, which is a hybrid between *L. latifolia* and *L. angustifolia*).

Syn. is an abbreviation for 'synonym', which refers to the fact that the plant is well known by, or may be sold under, an alternative name.

Award of Garden Merit

Throughout the directory section that follows, you will see the initials AGM set after certain plants. This denotes that the plant in question has passed certain assessments carried out by experts under the auspices of the Royal Horticultural Society in the UK. Only plants with exceptionally good garden qualities can be given this special Award of Garden Merit, and obtaining a plant with this distinction should give you a degree of guarantee and comfort. It is then up to you to make sure the plant you choose is appropriate to the situation, and that you give it the love and care that it deserves.

▼ *Lavandula stoechas* 'Anouk'

Achillea millefolium

Yarrow, milfoil

Description

T HE SPECIES most useful as a herb is *Achillea millefolium*, a pungent perennial with flat, cream–white to pink flower heads rising on sturdy stems 6–12in (15–30cm) high. The foliage is greyish–green and comprises finely divided leaves. Yarrow has creeping roots and efficient self-seeding, so once you have a plant or two, you will always have them; some gardeners consider these plants invasive. Yarrow is good for the organic gardener, since adding it – even one small leaf – to a compost heap is said to speed decomposition of the other ingredients. Also, the root secretions will activate the disease resistance of many nearby plants.

Recommended varieties

O RNAMENTAL CULTIVARS include *A. filipendulina* 'Gold Plate' AGM with small, golden flower heads, and the light yellow *A.* 'Moonshine' AGM. 'Alabaster' is pale yellow, fading to white; 'Bloodstone' is very deep red; 'Cassis' is a deep cherry red; 'Fanal' (sometimes found as 'The Beacon') opens bright red and fades to brownish–yellow; 'Feuerland' (or 'Fireland') opens to bright red–orange, fading attractively to orange and yellow.

▼ *Achillea* **'Feuerland'**

How to grow

USDA zone Z2–3
Site Full sun, but tolerates light shade.
Soil Moderately rich and moist.
Propagation By division in spring or autumn.
Growing The straight species can be invasive so when grown as a garden plant keep it in a container, or restrict the roots by surrounding them with tiles pushed into the soil.
Harvesting Collect leaves and flowers in late summer.

Known uses

Ornamental appeal Useful border plant. Display the dried flower heads indoors.
Culinary Finely chop the slightly bitter, peppery-tasting young leaves into salads and soft cheese dips. English mace (*Achillea ageratum*) is a little-grown culinary herb with a mildly spicy flavour, used in chicken dishes, soups, stews and sauces.
Cosmetic A weak infusion of the flowering tops in distilled water makes a cleanser or refreshing toner for oily skin.
Medicinal Taken as a tea it can relieve colds and fever. It is also thought to lower blood pressure and aid digestion. The essential oil contains azulene, which has anti-inflammatory properties. Apply externally for ulcers, wounds and nose bleeds (a common name for *Achillea* in some parts is 'nose bleed').
Household None.

Ajuga reptans
Bugle

Description

AJUGAS MAKE excellent ground-cover plants. A hardy, often vigorous plant that flowers in spring or early summer, it comes in a wide range of forms with coloured and variegated foliage.

Recommended varieties

AJUGA REPTANS produces flowers of royal blue over deep green leaves. Varieties bred for their rich leaf colourings include 'Arctic Fox' (cream leaves with dark green edges) and 'Braunherz' (deep purple bronze); both grow to just 6in (15cm) or so in height.

How to grow

USDA zone Z6
Site Full sun to dappled shade.
Soil A moist, relatively strongly acidic soil.
Propagation Sow seed in autumn (or spring as a second choice); divide from rooted runners in autumn or spring.
Growing It does not attract pests and diseases generally, therefore it is good for the organic gardener. It can be invasive.
Harvesting Gather leaves and flowers in early summer (for medicinal usage).

▼ *Ajuga* **'Braunherz'**

Alchemilla mollis AGM
Lady's mantle

Description

THIS PLANT has green foliage and yellow-green, feathery sprays of flowers that last for several weeks. *Alchemilla* self-seeds, so it may crop up in other places in the garden.

Recommended varieties

ALCHEMILLA MOLLIS AGM is the form most commonly found. 'Robusta' is slightly taller, up to 30in (75cm) and 'Variegata' has leaves that are accented with yellow markings.

How to grow

USDA zone Z5–7
Site Light shade is preferred.
Soil Slightly acidic, moist.
Propagation Sow seed in spring or autumn.
Growing Easy to grow and seeds itself anywhere.
Harvesting Cut young leaves any time during the growing season , after the dew has dried. Harvest for drying as the plant comes into flower.

▼ *Alchemilla mollis* **AGM**

Allium
Chive, garlic, onion

Description

ONIONS GROWING in the vegetable garden are one thing, and ornamental species in the flower garden are another. However, there are also some forms of *Allium* that are most at home in the herb garden. Vegetable alliums are, of course, the onion, shallot, leek and garlic, whereas the decorative alliums (which comprise dozens of species) are grown for their round flower heads comprising masses of short, tubular flowers in shades of blue, purple, pink or white, and occasionally yellow. In the herb garden the main types of alliums are chives (*A. schoenopraesum*) and garlic (*A. sativum*), but there are others. In general, alliums have long leaves, either thick or strap-shaped, which sometimes die down before the flowers appear. Chives have cylindrical leaves and a mild onion flavour. The mid-summer flowers are globular and mauve. Garlic produces flat, solid leaves and white flowers.

Recommended varieties

CHINESE CHIVES (*A. tuberosum*) produce white, starry, sweet-scented flowers in late summer, with flat, green leaves. They have a mild garlic flavour and a tuberous root. The Welsh onion (*A. fistulosum*) carries white flowers in summer and strong-flavoured, evergreen leaves. The everlasting onion (*A. cepa*) is an 'ever-ready' perennial producing sharp-flavoured 'spring' onions; it rarely flowers. The tree or Egyptian onion (*A. cepa* var. *proliferum*) produces small pickling onions on the tips of the stems; this variety can grow to 3ft (1m) or so and may need staking. The giant garlic or rocambole (*A. scorodoprasum*) is a mild, garlic-flavoured bulb, producing mauve flowers and edible bulbs at the tips of the stems. Finally there is the wild or wood garlic, also known as ramsons (*A. ursinium*), which is usually found growing wild in light woodland; it carries loose,

▼ *Allium schoenoprasum*   ▼ *Allium schoenoprasum*   ▼ *Allium ursinium*

starry white flowers in late spring. This last species may prove invasive and is best confined to a wild part of the garden since it can rapidly become a weed in more cultivated garden areas.

How to grow

USDA zone Z5–9
Site Choose a sunny corner of the garden to grow them, or a large pot in a sunny spot on the patio or balcony.
Soil Any soil will do, but it should be dug well before planting. Sprinkle a handful of organic general fertilizer, such as seaweed, or blood, fish and bone.
Propagation Sow seed in spring, or plant prepared onion 'sets' in the spring or autumn. In the case of garlic, take a bulb and split it into its clove sections, planting these just under the surface of the soil. Divide and replant clumps of chives every three to four years. You can pot some up in autumn for indoor windowsill cropping over winter.
Growing Onions generally need to grow 9in (23cm) apart; garlic can be 6in (15cm) apart. Water all onions during dry spells. Feed chives monthly during the growing season.

▼ *Allium sativum*

Known uses

Ornamental appeal Decorative alliums are useful in the flower border and containers, whereas all other onions are better placed in the vegetable or herb garden. Dried onion flower heads are used in arranging.
Culinary The florets from chive flower heads can be sprinkled on salads. Chopped chive leaves are used in salads, sandwiches and soups. Garlic bulbs should be used sparingly; rub the clove around salads bowls to add flavour. Chewing parsley or cardamom seed will counteract garlic breath. Pickle tree, everlasting and Welsh onions in wine vinegar.
Cosmetic None.
Medicinal Alliums contain iron and vitamins, and are a mild antibiotic. Chives promote digestion and stimulate appetite, and are also a mild laxative. Garlic can be used as an antibiotic; it is also believed to 'cleanse' blood, reduce blood pressure and clear catarrh. It is sometimes taken as protection against common colds, as well as worms, typhoid and dysentery.
Household Garlic, grown in pots (or stored as bulbs) and kept indoors near to house plants, will deter aphids and whitefly from infesting those plants.

Harvesting With chives, cut the leaves leaving the bottom 2in (5cm) or so for regrowth. If the flowers are removed (rather than kept and enjoyed), the remaining leaves have a better flavour. With garlic, dig up the clustered bulbs in late summer; handle them gently to avoid bruising.

Aloe vera AGM

Aloe vera

Description

To most non–gardeners, *Aloe vera* is best known as an ingredient in many toiletries. However, it is an attractive plant for the patio or home though it is not really suitable for planting out in borders or the herb garden as it looks incongruous and is not completely hardy. Its ornamental appeal is that it produces a rosette of tapering, toothed, thick, fleshy, typically succulent, green leaves. Occasionally these leaves are flecked with darker or lighter markings, or they may be an all–over, plain, grey–green shade. Sometimes a plant will flower, but this is not a given. When it does, it sends out a spike of very slender, trumpet–shaped, yellow-orange flowers. Remove this at the base when it dies.

Recommended varieties

Aloe vera AGM is the only species of *Aloe* recommended for its herbal properties, although there are a number of other species and cultivars grown as decorative garden and container plants.

▼ **Aloe vera AGM**

How to grow

USDA zone Z8
Site Full sun, sheltered from cold winds.
Soil Free–draining, fertile soil, preferably low in organic matter. If growing in a container, use a good quality, soil–based potting compost.
Propagation By removal of offsets.
Growing Do not mulch as this may give rise to crown–rotting. Water regularly in summer, but allow to dry out between waterings. Apply a weak, organic, liquid fertilizer (such as seaweed), monthly during the growing season.
Harvesting Cut leaves as needed; the best leaves are from plants at least two years old.

Known uses

Ornamental appeal Arguably better in a container that can be moved under cover when harsh weather is forecast. Can be grown successfully as a house plant.
Culinary None.
Cosmetic *Aloe vera* is the basis of a number of skin products.
Medicinal The sap, when fresh, is applied and used to soothe and heal burned or otherwise damaged skin. Be warned, however, that there are several other forms of *Aloe* that are sold as ornamental garden plants, and these can contain astringent sap. Therefore use only *Aloe vera* for soothing damaged skin.
Household None, but the closely related *Aloe perryi* gives a rich violet-coloured dye.

Aloysia triphylla AGM
Lemon verbena

Description

THIS SOUTH American native has probably the most lemony scent of any plant other than a lemon. It belongs to the same family as the flowering *Verbena* (found in hundreds of hanging baskets during summer), but it is in a different genus, and it is certainly less aesthetically pleasing. The leaves are long and pointed, and are arranged on the stem in sets of three. The flowers are tiny, white and pale purple, and carried in loose clusters at the tops of the stems in late summer.

Recommended varieties

NORMALLY ONLY the species is available. This plant may also be found under its old name of *Lippia citriodora*.

How to grow

USDA zone Z8
Site Full sun; shelter from cold winds.
Soil Free-draining, preferably slightly alkaline.
Propagation By softwood cuttings in late spring or early summer, in a covered propagator with some slight bottom heat. Or sow seeds in spring.
Growing Mulch in autumn to protect the roots from winter frost. In cold areas prune the plant back in late autumn and cover the root area with straw. In very cold areas it is best to grow the plants in containers and move them under cover for the winter. New growth can appear late, so do not lift and discard plants until you are sure they are dead – probably by late summer.
Harvesting Pick leaves throughout the growing season; the lemon scent is at its best just as the flowers begin to bloom.

Known uses

Ornamental appeal A fairly plain plant so not ideal for the flower border – but a must for the herb garden.
Culinary Use the leaves in herbal teas; chop the leaves to add a lemon flavour to desserts and confectionery.
Cosmetic Used as the basis of many skin creams. Macerate in almond oil for a massage. Make an infusion and allow to cool, then use to reduce puffiness around the eyes (soak cotton wool in the infusion and place over eyes for 15 minutes).
Medicinal A mildly sedative tea can be made, and is believed to soothe bronchial and nasal congestion (as well as nausea, stomach cramps and flatulence).
Household Use in pot-pourri, linen sachets and herb pillows.

▼ *Aloysia triphylla* **AGM**

Anethum graveolens
Dill

Description

DILL IS a hardy annual. It has hollow stems and feathery, finely divided leaves. In mid–summer its aromatic, yellow flowers are carried in umbrella–shaped ('umbel') heads. These are followed by brown, ridged, aromatic seeds.

Recommended varieties

THE BASIC dill species is *Anethum graveolens*. The cultivar 'Bouquet', with its many branches and compact flower heads, is popular for its seed production. The cultivar 'Fernleaf' is shorter–growing, at just 18in (45cm) in height, making it more suitable for containers. It also has attractive, dark blue–green leaves.

How to grow

USDA zone Z9–11
Site Full sun to light shade; it is better in a sheltered spot.
Soil A light, medium–rich soil with plenty of moisture.
Propagation Sow seed in spring in shallow drills where it is to grow, in rows 12in (30cm) apart. Thin to 9in (23cm). A second mid–summer sowing will produce a further supply in autumn. Dill also self–seeds freely.
Growing Support the plants with canes as they grow. Water well during the growing season, as dill can run to seed if it becomes too dry. Discard plants in autumn.
Harvesting Harvest leaves just before the plant comes into flower. Collect and dry the seeds after the flower heads turn brown.

Known uses

Ornamental appeal It is obviously good in the herb garden; in the flower border less so. It makes a decorative container plant for the patio.
Culinary Add the flowering tops to pickles, boil the leaves with new potatoes, and use the seeds in bread, soups and fish dishes.
Cosmetic Crush and infuse the seed for use in a nail-strengthening bath.
Medicinal Use in a salt-free diet, as dill is rich in mineral salts. Make dill water to provide relief from indigestion, hiccups, colic, flatulence and insomnia. Chew seed to sweeten the breath.
Household None.

▼ *Anethum graveolens* **'Bouquet'**

Angelica archangelica
Angelica

Description

THIS IS a moisture–loving plant with large, glossy, deeply indented leaves. The stems can grow to some 7ft (2m) high, and 30in (75cm) wide. The stems have a distinctly pink or brownish tinge. Umbels of small, greenish–white flowers held above the leaves appear in summer.

Recommended varieties

NORMALLY ONLY the species is grown, although there are some 30 or so forms commonly available.

How to grow

USDA zone Z7
Site Angelica prefers a position in partial shade.
Soil Any moist, fertile soil.
Propagation Sow seed in late summer (the seeds quickly lose their viability). Sow outdoors directly; plants in the herb garden that are allowed to flower will give rise to many seedlings.

▼ *Angelica archangelica*

Known uses

Ornamental appeal Not especially attractive for the ornamental garden. The dried seed heads make a striking winter decoration.
Culinary The stems are crystallized for decorating cakes. Leaves are used in compotes of rhubarb and other fruits to reduce acidity. The seeds are used to flavour gin and other drinks.
Cosmetic Leaves can be added to a bath for increased relaxation.
Medicinal Make a tea from the leaves as a tonic for colds and to reduce flatulence. Crushed leaves seem to reduce the symptoms of car sickness.
Household The roots can be used as a source of a pleasant, sweet aroma in the home (they have the longest-lasting aroma of any part of the plant). Chopped pieces of root can be added to pot-pourris, or the essential oil from them can be used as a pot-pourri fixative.

Growing Best grown as a biennial: sow seed in growing positions in spring, cut down to soil level in autumn and then mulch. Sowing can also be carried out in late summer for harvesting the following year. Give a light dressing of general organic fertilizer in the spring.
Harvesting Harvest leaves in early summer, then the stems and the seed heads in late summer. The roots are best if they are lifted during the first autumn (after a spring sowing), or in the second autumn (after a late summer sowing), at which point the plant should be discarded.

Anthriscus cerefolium
Chervil

Description

THIS HERB looks more like the kind of plant you will see growing wild by the roadside in rural areas – indeed it is closely related to the white–flowered cow parsley that does grow there. For this reason the herb has often been overlooked as a valuable garden plant. But it does have a valid place in the herb garden, and is increasingly being used for its parsley–like flavour with a hint of myrrh; it is commonly used in French cuisine. Very finely divided, mid–green leaves and white flower heads grow in a rather neat overall habit. Plants only grow to some 24in (60cm) in height.

Recommended varieties

NORMALLY THE straight species is grown.

How to grow

USDA zone Z9–11
Site Light shade in summer; full sun in winter (therefore a position under a deciduous tree could be ideal).
Soil Light and well drained.
Propagation For a regular supply, sow seed from mid–spring to late autumn.
Growing Although this herb is hardy, covering plants with cloches in winter will guarantee leaves for picking. It makes a good indoor plant, given adequate humidity and a bright place.
Harvesting Gather leaves before the flowers appear; do not pick from plants under 4in (10cm) in height as they will struggle to develop.

Known uses

Ornamental appeal Good for the herb garden, but not really anywhere else (in terms of its ornamental appeal).
Culinary Use leaves in salads, sauces and soups, as well as with chicken, fish and egg dishes. Add the chopped leaves near to the end of the cooking to avoid flavour loss. The stems can also be chopped for salads, soups and casseroles.
Cosmetic Infuse the leaves to make a face mask to cleanse skin and maintain suppleness; some people believe that it discourages wrinkles.
Medicinal Infuse in tea to stimulate digestion and to relieve chronic catarrh. Chervil is high in vitamin C, iron, magnesium and carotene, and was traditionally taken as a restorative tonic following periods of abstinence.
Household None.

▼ *Anthriscus cerefolium*

Armoracia rusticana

Horseradish

Description

L ARGE, STRAP−LIKE, fresh green leaves are the main feature of this culinary herb. It is a hardy herbaceous perennial. Small, quite insignificant, white flowers are produced, somewhat unpredictably, on tallish spikes in late summer. A vigorous grower, it is tenacious and invasive, so if you grow this plant – and you should – try to plant it in a pit lined with bricks or slabs (and preferably mortared, as the roots will always find their way out otherwise).

Recommended varieties

N ORMALLY THE straight species is grown. There is, however, *Armoracia rusticana* 'Variegata', a prettier variegated form with white leaf blotches. It does not seem to have any less culinary value.

▼ *Armoracia rusticana*

Known uses

Ornamental appeal Plant in the herb garden, or a wild area for regular cultivation.
Culinary Most famous for horseradish sauce (to accompany beef or fish dishes), made from the finely grated roots. The roots can also be grated into coleslaw, cream cheese and mayonnaise. Roots can be frozen, or preserved in vinegar. Young leaves can be added to salads.
Cosmetic Slice roots and infuse in milk to make a lotion to improve skin clarity.
Medicinal Grated root can be made into a poultice for applying to chilblains, rheumatic joints, stiff muscles and sciatica areas. Regular ingestion of grated horseradish will eliminate waste fluids and mucus. It can also be made into a syrup to relieve bronchitis and coughs.
Household None.

How to grow

USDA zone Z5
Site Any, but it prefers full sun.
Soil Any.
Propagation Take root cuttings in mid−winter or divide plants in spring. Seed is not generally available to buy.
Growing Grow in a pit, as described above. If this cannot be arranged, grow it in a part of the herb garden where it will not invade other plants.
Harvesting Dig the fresh roots for using at any time – but from established plants only. In the autumn dig up the roots for drying.

Artemisia
Southernwood, wormwood, French tarragon

Description

ALTHOUGH MANY will consider these to be shrubs, their wood is very light and some might well be better referred to as sub–shrubs. They can sometimes be on the tender side, too. They are grown for their soft, filigreed foliage that varies in the 'silveriness' of its grey, sometimes inclining towards a blue cast. They are easy to grow.

Recommended varieties

ARTEMISIA ABSINTHIUM is the true wormwood, considered the most bitter of herbs after rue. 'Lambrook Silver' AGM at 3ft (1m) is a good cultivar. Look also for the hybrid 'Powis Castle' AGM, with very finely cut foliage. *A. abrotanum* AGM is the southernwood, the sweetest perennial artemisia with a hint of lemon. *A. ludoviciana* 'Silver Queen' AGM is willow–like with silvery leaves. *A. dracunculus* is the French tarragon, *A. dracunculoides* is the Russian tarragon, and these both have a green, not a silver–grey appearance. Mugwort (*A. lactiflora* AGM) has deeply cut leaves and plumes of fragrant, cream flowers in late summer.

▼ *Artemisia abrotanum AGM*　▼ *Artemisia dracunculus*

How to grow

USDA zone Z4–5
Site Full sun.
Soil Light and well drained.
Propagation Take semi–ripe cuttings in mid– to late summer. Sow seeds when available (Russian tarragon should be sown in spring).
Growing Cut wormwood and southernwood back to within 6in (15cm) of the ground in autumn or early spring, then mulch well.
Harvesting Southernwood – pick shoots for drying in mid–summer; wormwood – cut leaves for drying in mid–summer; tarragon – pick leaves for using fresh throughout the growing season. Tarragon does not dry well, but it makes a good herb vinegar.

Known uses

Ornamental appeal All of the silver artemisias make useful plants for borders, and both southernwood and wormwood will make neat, low hedges.
Culinary Tarragon leaves are used in many sauces, and go well with fish dishes, salad dressings, soups or eggs. Add them also to butter for vegetables, steaks and grilled fish. Russian tarragon is good on grilled meat.
Cosmetic None.
Medicinal Infuse tarragon as an appetite stimulant and general tonic. Not suitable for pregnant women.
Household Powder leaves of wormwood to make a moth repellant.

Borago officinalis

Borage

Description

BORAGE IS one of the essentials of any herb garden. It is a self–seeding annual, growing to a height of 18–30in (45–75cm). It makes a lot of floppy growth. Beautiful, small, single, pointed flowers of electric blue, with black anthers, are carried from early summer onwards.

Recommended varieties

THE NORMAL species is the one to grow although there is a white form, 'Alba', and a rare form, 'Bill Archer', with variegated foliage.

How to grow

USDA zone Z7
Site Full sun.
Soil Any soil; borage is not suitable for growing in pots.

▽ **Borago officinalis**

Known uses

Ornamental appeal Attractive in the flower border. Decorative both as a garden plant and when the flowers are sprinkled over salads. When burnt, the nitrate of potash content in borage emits sparks and slight pops and crackles, like fireworks.
Culinary Flowers can be separated from the stalks and used in salads and summer drinks. Young leaves, which have a mild cucumber-like taste, can also be used in salads.
Cosmetic Add borage to a face pack to treat dry skin.
Medicinal Use borage in a salt-free diet as it is rich in mineral salts.
Household None.

Propagation Sow seeds in mid–spring, where the plants are to grow. A second sowing can be made two months later for a succession of young leaves and flowers. Sporadic growth of self–sown seedlings should maintain this in future years.
Growing Easy to grow; but can be susceptible to aphids (and mildew if the plants dry out and become stressed). Space it well; it should be set at least 24in (60cm) away from other herbs or plants.
Harvesting Cut the young leaves fresh throughout summer (they do not dry well). Pick fresh flowers when they are just fully opened (for drying or freezing).

Buxus sempervirens AGM

Box

Calendula officinalis

Pot marigold

Description

BOX HAS masses of small, leathery, green, evergreen leaves. In some forms the leaves are rounded, and in others they have a distinct point, especially when young. But it is the aroma of the foliage when brushed against that is the real joy. *Buxus* makes very dense growth, meaning that it is perfect for training into topiary shapes, or hedging.

Description

THIS HARDY annual is called 'marigold' because its flowers resemble the typical hybrid marigold flowers of the *Tagetes* genus. But plants are distinguishable in that *Calendula* leaves are oval and slightly hairy, whereas *Tagetes* leaves are usually a darker green and are segmented or divided. Calendulas are, unlike *Tagetes*, fairly immune to slug and snail damage.

Recommended varieties

THE STRAIGHT species (*Buxus sempervirens* AGM) is easy to find but there are dozens of cultivated and specially bred varieties, with some fine variegated forms, particularly *B. sempervirens* 'Elegantissima' AGM.

Recommended varieties

CALENDULA OFFICINALIS is the commonly grown species, with bright orange, single flowers. The following cultivars are well worth growing: 'Art Shades Mixed', 'Greenheart Orange' and 'Daisy Mixed'.

How to grow

USDA zone Z5
Site Full sun to medium shade.
Soil Rich, fertile soil; it prefers a slightly alkaline soil.
Propagation Take stem cuttings in spring.
Growing Water well whenever the soil is dry, and feed with a general organic fertilizer in spring. Keep trimmed to encourage dense, tight growth.
Harvesting Gather the leaves in spring, before flowering starts.

How to grow

USDA zone Z6–9
Site Full sun.
Soil It prefers a slightly acidic, well-drained soil.
Propagation Sow in autumn for flowering the following summer; or sow in spring.
Growing Keep soil moist; remove dead flowers regularly. Treat as an annual or biennial bedding plant and discard after flowering.
Harvesting Pick the flowers when they are open, and use them fresh or dried; the best leaves are picked when young.

◢ **Buxus sempervirens AGM**

◢ **Calendula 'Daisy Mixed'**

Carum carvi
Caraway

Description

CARAWAY IS hugely popular as a culinary herb; its seeds are recommended in a great many recipes and are readily available at food stores. It is, actually, an ancient herb, originally from the warmer reaches of Europe and Asia, and for this reason can be tricky to overwinter in cooler countries. In appearance it is very much like its relatives the umbellifers (closely related to parsley), with relatively low-growing, feathery green foliage and white flower heads in summer. It has an upright growth habit on stems that are just 18in (45cm) high.

Recommended varieties

NORMALLY ONLY the straight species is grown.

▼ *Carum carvi*

Known uses

Ornamental appeal Looking like a weed, the only place for this plant is the herb garden.
Culinary Seeds are traditionally used in cakes and bread, and with some pickles and cheeses. Important in Indian and Asian cuisine. Leaves may be used in salads and some say the roots can be boiled as a vegetable like its relative, the carrot.
Cosmetic An essential oil made from the seed is used in mouthwashes and colognes.
Medicinal Chewing the seed raw, or taking infused seed will aid digestion, sweeten breath (after eating garlic, for example), promote appetite and relieve flatulence.
Household None.

How to grow

USDA zone Z3
Site Full sun.
Soil Fertile, well-drained soil.
Propagation Best grown as a hardy annual: sow seed in late spring, where the plants are to grow, or sow in pots in autumn for transplanting into the herb garden the following spring.
Growing After germination the seedlings should be thinned to some 8in (20cm) apart. Not really suitable for growing in patio containers.
Harvesting Gather leaves when young. Pick seed heads in late summer or when the seeds have turned brown.

Chamaemelum nobile

Chamomile

Description

CHAMOMILE IS commonly used as a lawn substitute. You cannot, of course, mow a chamomile lawn in the same way as a grass lawn, and achieve neat, straight edges and stripes. Instead a chamomile lawn should be a small informal area for light foot traffic. The beauty of it is that as you walk across it, it throws up a wonderful fresh apple aroma. Even if you do not want a lawn of it, chamomile should be grown in the herb garden for its very soft, feathery foliage and low–growing habit above which the small, individual daisy flowers are carried.

Recommended varieties

'FLORE PLENO' has double daisy flowers. The cultivar 'Treneague' has apple–scented leaves and is flowerless, and therefore better for a lawn.

▼ *Chamaemelum nobile* **'Treneague'**

How to grow

USDA zone Z4
Site Full sun.
Soil Light and well drained.
Propagation Sow seed in spring (except for 'Treneague'); take 3in (8in) cuttings from side shoots in summer, or divide in spring or autumn. 'Treneague' can be propagated by cuttings or division.
Growing To make a lawn, plants need to be set out 4–6in (10–15cm) apart.
Harvesting Gather leaves any time. Pick flowers when they are fully open.

Known uses

Ornamental appeal Low-growing plants for patio containers, or as an aromatic substitute lawn.
Culinary None.
Cosmetic Infuse the flowers for use as a facial steam bath, and as a hand soak, to soften and whiten skin. A chamomile-flower eyebath can reduce inflammation and eliminate fatigue shadows. Boil the flowers (for 20 minutes or so) to use as a rinse to condition and lighten fair hair; this will need to be done regularly to be noticeable.
Medicinal Infuse flowers as a tea for a general tonic and sedative (good for calming down children and reducing the incidence of nightmares).
Household Use the aromatic flowers and leaves in pot-pourri.

Chenopodium bonus-henricus
Good King Henry

Description

WHY THIS has its common name is a mystery, but this is a species of plant that has been cultivated for centuries, and it both looks and tastes rather like spinach. It's a plant that straddles the boundary between herbs and vegetables. It produces arrow–shaped leaves of dark green, with a white mealy underside, and tiny greenish–yellow flowers in early summer.

Recommended varieties

NORMALLY ONLY the species is available.

How to grow

USDA zone Z5
Site Prefers full sun but will tolerate light shade.
Soil Rich, well–drained loam.
Propagation Sow seed in the spring where it is to grow; divide roots – preferably every two years – during autumn.
Growing Apply a balanced, organic, general fertilizer in spring; keep well watered during summer. Cut down most of the top growth and mulch in autumn.
Harvesting Allow plants to develop for a year and then pick leaves as required. Harvest the flowering spikes as they begin to open.

Known uses

Ornamental appeal It is better suited to the vegetable or herb garden (or allotment) rather than the ornamental garden.
Culinary Steam-cook the leaves like spinach, and the young flower heads like broccoli. Young leaves can be used fresh in salads and sandwiches.
Cosmetic None.
Medicinal A poultice and ointment made from the leaves can be used to cleanse and heal skin sores.
Household None.

Chenopodium bonus-henricus

Claytonia perfoliata
Winter purslane

Description

ALSO KNOWN as miner's lettuce, this plant is a succulent–like, hardy annual and deserves more attention as a salad herb. During spring it grows quickly, producing small white flowers on long stalks. The first–to–open leaves are narrow, while later leaves are rounded and become almost wrapped around the stem.

Recommended varieties

NORMALLY ONLY the species is found. May be found under its old name of *Montia*.

▼ **Claytonia perfoliata**

How to grow

USDA zone Z6
Site Full sun to light shade.
Soil Any soil.
Propagation Sow sequentially in growing positions from spring; for winter use, sow very thinly in rows in late summer.
Growing The plants need protection in a severe winter. When plants run to seed and die in mid–summer, leave a few to seed themselves. Then transplant the seedlings that autumn, or the following spring for a summer crop.
Harvesting Depending on the timing of the crop – harvest the leaves, stalks and flowers as they are required.

Known uses

Ornamental appeal It is not particularly decorative; it looks more like a weed and, to many gardeners, it probably is. Grown only in the kitchen or herb garden as a salad herb.
Culinary A typical cut-and-come-again crop, it provides cool 'bulk' in winter and early-spring salads. The stalks, leaves and flowers are all edible, and the leaves can be cooked like spinach.
Cosmetic None.
Medicinal High in vitamin C, and has been used in the treatment of scurvy (with its close relatives in the *Montia* and *Portulaca* genera).
Household None.

Coriandrum sativum
Coriander

Description

A HARDY ANNUAL, coriander grows to a height of 12–18in (30–45cm). It has an intriguing dual–foliage look, with fine, feathery, upper leaves and then broader, more parsley-like, lower ones. Plants have an upright growth habit and typical white, umbellifer flower heads in summer.

Recommended varieties

NORMALLY THE straight species is grown. Two other plants with coriander in their name are Vietnamese coriander (*Persicaria odorata*, in the *Polygonum* or knotweed family), which has a lemon–coriander scent and is added to meat dishes; and the Roman coriander (*Nigella sativa*, in the *Ranunculus* or buttercup family), used to flavour bread, sauces, chutneys and curries.

How to grow

USDA zone Z10–11
Site A sunny, sheltered position.
Soil A light, free–draining soil.
Propagation Sow seed in late spring in the position where it is to grow.
Growing Thin plants out if they are being grown for their seed; successive sowings can be made for closely spaced leaf crops.
Harvesting Cut broad young seedling leaves for fresh use; they do not dry well. Gather seeds when they have turned brown.

▼ **The feathery upper leaves and white flowers of coriander**

▼ **The broader, more parsley-like, lower leaves**

Known uses

Ornamental appeal Slightly more attractive than its close relatives chervil and caraway, but still only really suited to the vegetable or herb garden.
Culinary Young leaves used mostly in Indian cuisine. Seeds are ground and used in spicy, savoury and sweet dishes.
Cosmetic None.
Medicinal Chew seeds or infuse as a tea to be used as a digestive tonic and mild sedative. Add an essential oil to ointments for painful rheumatic joints and muscles.
Household Use the seed in pot-pourri.

Foeniculum vulgare

Herb fennel

Description

EVERY PART of herb fennel, from the seed to the root, is edible. The leaves are aromatic, finely cut and lime–green turning dark green by autumn. The flowers are small, aromatic, flat, yellow clusters carried at the ends of stems in mid–summer. Growing to a height of 5–7ft (1.5–2m), fennel is a big plant – very big if you consider the small amount of it that you need in cooking (as its aniseed–like flavour is so strong).

Recommended varieties

FOR HERBAL use, choose the normal green species, but there is also the increasingly popular, bronze–leaved variant (*Foeniculum vulgare* var. *purpurascens*). Florence fennel or finnocchio (*F. vulgare* var. *dulce*) is grown for its aniseed–flavoured, swollen leaf bases or 'bulbs'; the ferny foliage can also be used as a garnish.

How to grow

USDA zone Z5
Site If you wish for the seed to be ripened, a site in full sun is required, otherwise fennel can tolerate partial shade.

▼ *Foeniculum vulgare var. purpurascens*

Soil Herb fennel prefers a chalky soil, whilst Florence fennel grows better in a quite strongly acidic soil.
Propagation Sow seed between late spring and early summer; fennel self–sows once established. Divide plants in autumn.
Growing Thin seedlings so they are 20in (50cm) apart. Remove faded flower heads if the seed is not required, as this will give better leaf production. Do not grow fennel near to coriander as it reduces the seed production of the fennel, and do not grow fennel near to dill as the flowers will cross–pollinate, which compromises the successful production of seed for both.
Harvesting Pick young leaves and stems as needed. Collect seed when it is ripe.

Known uses

Ornamental appeal A must for the herb garden, herb fennel is also an attractive border plant (towards the back, owing to its height). Florence fennel is only appropriate for the herb or vegetable garden.
Culinary Chopped leaves and seed give an aniseed flavour to salads, sauces, soups and fish dishes. Stems, if tender, can be chopped and added to salads, too.
Cosmetic Use seeds and leaves in facial steam baths for deep cleansing. Chew the seed to sweeten breath.
Medicinal Fennel seed can reduce the toxic effect of alcohol on the body. Infuse it as a tea to aid digestion and relieve constipation. Chew seed to allay hunger.
Household None.

Glycyrrhiza glabra
Liquorice

Description

L IQUORICE IS a hardy herbaceous perennial principally grown by commercial growers, for the confectionary and medicinal value of its thick tap roots. In the garden, however, it does offer cool, ferny, dark green foliage and blue, purple or white sweet pea-like flowers in summer. These are followed by reddish-brown seed pods. Typically the plant reaches a height of between 2–5ft (60–150cm).

Recommended varieties

N ORMALLY ONLY the species is available.

How to grow

USDA zone Z8
Site Full sun.
Soil It prefers a deep, moist, rich sandy loam.
Propagation Divide roots in autumn or spring.
Growing Cut down the foliage in autumn, and mulch annually in spring.
Harvesting Lift three-year-old roots in late summer or early autumn.

Glycyrrhiza glabra

Helichrysum italicum AGM
Curry plant

Description

H ELICHRYSUM IS a large genus of perennials some of which are woody, and therefore classed as sub-shrubs. The curry plant (*H. italicum* AGM) smells exactly of curry powder, but it comes from southern Europe, far from the Indian continent. It has silver, needle-like leaves with heads of tiny, yellow button flowers in summer. It grows to some 18–24in (45–60cm) in height.

Recommended varieties

H . *MICROPHYLLUM* is almost the same, but has smaller leaves.

How to grow

USDA zone Z7–10
Site Full sun.
Soil It prefers a light, free-draining, moderately rich, acidic soil.
Propagation Take semi-ripe cuttings in summer, rooting them in a gritty, soil-based compost.
Growing Mulch in autumn and spring, and give a dressing of a balanced, organic, general fertilizer in early spring. Trim plants lightly in early spring to remove winter-damaged shoots and to maintain a neat shape.
Harvesting Pick leaves at any time of year. Pick the flowers as required in summer.

Helichrysum italicum **AGM**

Hyssopus officinalis

Hyssop

Description

ONE OF the best-known of garden herbs, hyssop has many uses as well as ornamental appeal; it also has a number of colourful forms (blue, pink and white). It is a member of the Lamiaceae plant family (sharing with the likes of sage, lavender and wall germander), and in its basic species, spikes of small, blue, lavender-like flowers appear on neat, rather bushy plants 30in (75cm) or so high. The dark green leaves are narrow, up to 1in (2.5cm) long, and very aromatic.

Recommended varieties

THE NORMAL blue-flowered species is widely available, but selected forms are offered as *Hyssopus officinalis* f. *albus* (white), and 'Roseus' (pink). Rock hyssop (*H. officinalis* subsp. *aristatus*) is a compact cultivar 12in (30cm) high; it produces blue-purple flowers and aromatic leaves.

How to grow

USDA zone Z3
Site Full sun.
Soil Light, well drained and slightly alkaline.
Propagation Sow species types in spring. Take stem cuttings from spring to autumn. Divide roots in spring.
Growing If grown as low hedging, plants should be set 12in (30cm) apart, otherwise twice this distance is sufficient for normal growing. Cut plants back annually in spring or, if you live in a mild winter area, after flowering. Hyssop can be grown in pots indoors.
Harvesting Cut young leaves and flowers for drying in the summer. Flowers should be picked when they are fully opened. The fragrance is generally improved with drying.

Known uses

Ornamental appeal Hyssop is a plant best reserved for the middle part of a border, or herb garden, because although it is good enough to be noticed, it does not bear close scrutiny, as would be the case right at the front of the border.
Culinary The flowers can be tossed into salads. Leaves can be used in a wide range of meat and fish dishes, especially stronger-tasting dishes such as game (rub leaves on skin), rich pâté, rabbit pie, lamb stews and so on. They also go well with cranberries in fruit salads and in fruit pies.
Cosmetic None.
Medicinal Infuse flowers as a tea for lung and throat complaints and bronchial congestion. Leaves can be used in poultices to heal bruises and wounds.
Household None.

▼ *Hyssopus officinalis*

Laurus nobilis AGM
Bay or **sweet bay**

Description

BAY IS a slow-growing tree native to the Mediterranean region. It has smooth, shiny, leathery, deep green leaves that dry well. They also have a pungent, eucalyptus-like smell. Small yellowish flowers appear in late spring that, on the female plant, are followed by glossy, blackish berries. If left to its own devices, a bay can grow to around 30ft (9m), but in most gardens it is kept smaller by trimming, and is often seen trained into standards or geometric shapes (topiary).

Recommended varieties

THE STRAIGHT species is most commonly grown, but there are a few worthwhile variants. The willow leaf bay (*Laurus nobilis* f. *angustifolia*) is slightly shorter at 23ft (7m) and has narrower leaves. The golden bay (*L. nobilis* 'Aurea' AGM) is shorter still at 16ft (5m), and has pale golden leaves (which, to me, can look somewhat insipid rather than attractive).

▼ *Laurus nobilis* **AGM**

Known uses

Ornamental appeal As specimen trees in borders or in lawns; can be grown as trained topiary and hedging in sheltered areas.
Culinary Use the leaves to add flavour to soups, stews, sauces and stocks. Add them, also, to poached fish, and put them on the coals of a barbecue. They can be boiled in milk to flavour rice pudding and custard, and they can be put into jars of rice to add flavour. An essential ingredient of bouquet garni.
Cosmetic None.
Medicinal An infusion of leaves will aid digestion and increase appetite, and can be added to a bath to relieve aching limbs.
Household Can be placed into bags of flour to deter flour weevils.

How to grow

USDA zone Z7–9
Site Shelter is more important than sunlight; it will tolerate partial shade, but not fierce winds.
Soil Light, well-drained soil.
Propagation Not easy. Viable seed is virtually impossible to obtain. Softwood cuttings (with a 'heel') can be taken in spring, or semi-ripe cuttings in late summer, and placed in pots in a cold frame.
Growing If you live in a cold area, grow bay in a container and overwinter it under cover.
Harvesting Leaves can be taken all year round.

Lavandula
Lavender

Description

ORIGINALLY FROM southern Europe and the Mediterranean region, lavender is widely grown purely as an ornamental perennial sub–shrub. It has a camphoraceous scent but sometimes with more of a balsam– or lemon–like aroma. Plants grow to some 28in (70cm) in height and spread. The foliage is greyish–green, and the flowers purplish–blue, appearing on spikes from mid–summer to mid–autumn. The stems become woody after a few years, making it best to replace plants after three or four years. The name 'lavender' comes from the lavender water that is made from the oil distilled from the plants, *lavo* being Latin for 'wash'.

Recommended varieties

THE OLD English lavender (*Lavandula angustifolia*) has pale blue flowers on long stems. There are some 60 cultivars available, including 'Alba' (white), 'Hidcote' AGM (with violet flowers), 'Hidcote Pink' (pink), 'Imperial Gem' AGM (deep violet), 'Loddon Blue' AGM (violet–blue), 'Munstead' (lavender–blue), 'Royal Purple' (deep purple) and 'Twickel Purple' (violet–blue). The lavendin (*L. x intermedia*) is a variable species, generally producing large, robust plants – to 32in (80cm) in height – with a rounded habit, but with branching stems. The main species has light blue to violet flowers that are very fragrant. The French lavender (*L. stoechas* AGM) is very popular. It has dark purple flowers borne in dense, congested heads topped by distinctive terminal bracts. There are some 30 cultivars commonly available; look for 'Anouk' (deep purple with pale purple bracts), 'Kew Red' (magenta and pink), and 'Snowman' (white). Another beauty is *L. pedunculata* subsp. *pedunculata* 'James Compton' (purple and bright red–violet). There are also several dozen hybrids, some of the best including 'Ballerina' (purple and pale pink), 'Helmsdale' (deep purple) and 'Regal Splendour' (violet–purple and rose pink).

▼ *Lavandula stoechas* **AGM**

▼ *Lavandula stoechas* **'Anouk'**

▼ *Lavandula* **'Ballerina'**

How to grow

USDA zone Z3
Site Open, sunny position to discourage fungal diseases.
Soil Well-drained neutral to alkaline soil. *L. stoechas*, however, does particularly well in acid soil.
Propagation Take semi-ripe cuttings in summer. Sow seed in spring. *L. angustifolia* germinates better, and more quickly, if the seed is placed in the freezer for a few hours before sowing. Cultivars do not come true from seed.
Growing Trim hedges and cut specimen plants back in spring to encourage bushiness. Deadhead and trim lightly after flowering. Pleasingly, the only pest likely to be visibly present will be the froghopper, which cocoons itself in frothy blobs of liquid known as cuckoo spit. This is a short-term presence, causing little damage to the plant, and the best course of action is to pick off the pests by hand.
Harvesting Flower heads or individual flowers can be gathered as they open, for drying. Leaves are picked at any time for use in pillows and sachets.

▼ *Lavandula* '**Helmsdale**'

Known uses

Ornamental appeal Lavenders make good specimen plants in borders and containers, and several plants together make good low, informal hedging. Add sprigs to wreaths and nosegays; arrange dried bunches on their own or with other small flowers.
Culinary Use the flowers to flavour jams, jellies, biscuits, butter, cream, sugar and vinegar. Flowers may be used, in small quantities, as an ingredient in fragrant stews. Leaf taste is bitter, but sometimes used in dishes from southern Europe.
Cosmetic Use flowers to make a tonic water (which is understood to speed cell replacement) for sensitive skin. Take a cup of lavender flowers and steep these for six days in an airtight jar containing a quarter of a cup of ethyl alcohol. Shake each day, and at the end, strain the fluid into a dark glass bottle. Use lavender oil in massage to ease muscular aches, cellulite and fluid retention.
Medicinal Infuse the flowers as a tea to calm nerves, soothe headaches, and ease dizziness, fainting, flatulence and halitosis. Neat essential oil of lavender is used as an antiseptic and mild sedative, and also as a painkiller (particularly on insect bites and stings or small burns).
Household Scent drawers and protect linen from moth attacks by making sachets or pillows of dried leaves and flowers. Fresh flowers rubbed onto skin, or pinned onto clothing, can discourage flies. Use dried stems as scented firelighters.

◄ *Lavandula stoechas* '**Regal Splendour**'

Levisticum officinale
Lovage

Description

LOVAGE GETS its name because it was used, back in the sixteenth century, as an aphrodisiac. It is a hardy perennial plant growing to some 6ft (2m) in height. Flat clusters of tiny, pale greenish–yellow flowers appear in summer, followed by brown seeds. The deeply divided, toothed leaves smell of celery when crushed. In fact, in France the name for lovage is 'false celery' because of this aroma and its flavour when used in the kitchen.

Recommended varieties

ONLY THE species is available.

How to grow

USDA zone Z4
Site Full sun or partial shade.
Soil Rich, well fed and well drained.
Propagation Sow seeds between spring and late summer. Divide established plants in spring.
Growing In autumn, after the plant has died back, feed well with well-rotted manure.
Harvesting Pick the main crop of fresh leaves before flowering; old leaves become tough and bitter. Harvest seeds as they turn brown.

Known uses

Ornamental appeal Good plant for the herb garden, and as a container plant to be kept near the kitchen door, but it is not generally considered decorative enough to use in the ornamental garden.
Culinary Add tender young leaves to salads. Crushed seeds can be used in bread, or rice and salads.
Cosmetic None.
Medicinal An infusion of the seed or leaf reduces water retention.
Household None.

▼ *Levisticum officinale*

Melissa officinalis
Lemon balm

Description

L EMON BALM is a hardy herbaceous perennial growing up to 30in (75cm) in height. Clusters of small, cream flowers are carried in summer; these flowers are rich in nectar and are therefore eagerly sought out by bees and butterflies. The leaves, which have a strong scent of lemon, are oval, toothed and textured.

Recommended varieties

G OLDEN LEMON balm (*Melissa officinalis* 'All Gold') is the same as the species except that the leaves are golden–yellow. Variegated lemon balm (*M. officinalis* 'Aurea') is variegated green and gold.

How to grow

USDA zone Z4
Site Full sun.
Soil Any soil, as long as it is not waterlogged in winter.
Propagation Sow seeds (main species only) in spring. Take softwood cuttings of any of the lemon balms in early summer. Divide established plants in early spring or early autumn.

Known uses

Ornamental appeal Useful plant for edging a border, as even the plain green leaves are quite attractive. Be careful, however, as the plant self-seeds and can be invasive. Lemon balm is good in containers.
Culinary The lemon scent is lost when cooked, so use the fresh young leaves raw in fruit salads.
Cosmetic Rub the leaf into the skin as a natural insect repellent.
Medicinal An infusion of leaves helps to lower fever and improves digestion. It is also a mild anti-depressant. It helps heal and prevent cold sores.
Household None.

Growing Immediately after flowering, cut plants back by around half. This will prevent the stems from becoming woody and straggly, stops the plant from seeding everywhere and encourages more fresh, young leaves.
Harvesting Pick fresh leaves before the flowers open; this is when the highest yield of leaf oil is available.

▼ *Melissa officinalis*

▼ *Melissa officinalis* 'All Gold'

▼ *Melissa officinalis* 'Aurea'

Mentha
Mint

Description

MINT IS arguably the best known of the culinary herbs, but its most ancient uses were medicinal. Egyptian tombs dating back 3,000 years have been found to contain mint, and the Japanese have been growing it to obtain menthol for more than 2,000 years. In general it has erect, square–shaped stems and toothed, bright green leaves, and it carries pinkish–lilac flowers in summer. These flowers are highly attractive to butterflies. Depending on the type of mint grown, it can reach anything from 12in (30cm) to 39in (1m) in height.

Recommended varieties

SPEARMINT (*MENTHA spicata*) is probably the most widely grown type, and for this reason it is also known simply as 'garden mint'. Peppermint (*M.* x *piperita*) has darkish leaves with a reddish tinge and is strongly peppermint–scented. The eau de cologne mint (*M. piperita* f. *citrata*), has smooth bergamot–scented, purple–tinged leaves and purple stems. Chocolate peppermint (*M. piperita* f. *citrata* 'Chocolate') has pointed, dark green–brown leaves with serrated edges; it is strongly peppermint–scented with deep chocolate undertones (making it great in puddings). Apple mint (*M. suaveolens*) has round, woolly leaves and a slight apple fragrance; it also has a variegated form, *M. suaveolens* 'Variegata' (but note that the common name for it is then pineapple mint rather than apple mint). Corsican mint (*M. requienii*) has tiny leaves and flowers and a creeping habit. Curly mint (*M. spicata* var. *crispa*) has leaves that are crinkled and have a slightly frilly edge. Ginger mint (*M.* x *gracilis*) is also known as Scotch mint, and has variegated gold and green leaves with serrated edges. Pennyroyal (*M. pulegium*) has bright green, peppermint–scented leaves. The odd

▼ *Mentha spicata*
var. *crispa*

▼ *Mentha* x *gracilis*

▼ *Mentha* x *piperita* f. *citrata*
'Lemon'

one out, of all the mint family, is the water mint (*M. aquatica*). It thrives in a wet soil, and is most at home in the margins of a pond, where its roots can be under water. Although technically an aquatic plant, its leaves can be used just like any other mint.

How to grow

USDA zone Z3–6
Site Partial shade, but mints will tolerate full sun.
Soil A moist, fertile soil.
Propagation Mint is very easy to propagate: take stem cuttings during the growing season, or root cuttings during the dormant season. It is not sensible to grow mint from seed as plants do not generally come true.
Growing It is best to sink mint into the ground in a bottomless bucket or pot to contain their tendency to spread. Mints are obvious subjects for growing in containers. They do need plenty of water, especially if in containers.
Harvesting Pick the leaves as required during the growing season; leaves can be used fresh, dried or frozen.

Known uses

Ornamental appeal All mints have attractive, fresh-looking leaves. Most are green, but there are plenty of delightful variegations (and other patterns) to choose. Small, purple and purple-mauve flowers are carried in summer. Essential for the herb garden, but be careful where you plant mint as it can be invasive.
Culinary A sprig of fresh mint is traditionally used in pots of boiling potatoes to add a subtle minty flavour. Chopped fresh leaves are good in a sauce with lamb. In truth, the delicate flavours of mint can be used with almost any dish – savoury or sweet – and experimenting is fun. Infusions, especially of peppermint, produce delicious tea.
Cosmetic Add spearmint and eau de cologne mint to make an invigorating and refreshing bath.
Medicinal The fragrance of mint (either fresh or from infusions) gives relief from headaches and nasal congestion. Peppermint is the most often used type for these purposes. Externally, peppermint oil can be used in a massage to relieve muscular pain.
Household Use leaf oil to overpower tobacco smells. Strew pennyroyal in cupboards and on soft furnishings to deter ants and fleas.

Mentha suaveolens

Mentha suaveolens '**Variegata**'

Mentha aquatica

Monarda

Bergamot, bee balm or Oswego tea

Description

THESE ARE beautiful plants with flamboyant flowers. In fact they are quite as likely to be seen growing in the ornamental garden as they are the herb garden. Bergamot usually has the fragrance of oranges. The leaves are bright green and narrowly elongated, and the flowers are rather spidery, in red, pink, purple or white, depending on the variety. The name Oswego tea comes from the use of wild bergamot (*Monarda fistulosa*) by the North American Oswego Indians.

Recommended varieties

THERE ARE more than 80 species and cultivars commonly available. The normal species (*Monarda didyma*) is a good herb plant but if you prefer rather more striking flowers, then choose 'Beauty of Cobham' AGM (pale pink), 'Cambridge Scarlet' AGM (scarlet) or 'Schneewittchen' (white).

How to grow

USDA zone Z4–6
Site Full sun to light shade.
Soil Rich, moist but not waterlogged soil.

Known uses

Ornamental appeal Good for the flower border as well as the herb garden; not very suited to growing in patio containers.
Culinary Flowers or young bergamot leaves can be used for a hint of orange flavour in salads or desserts.
Cosmetic The oil is used in perfumes.
Medicinal The tea, made from the leaves, is claimed to relieve colds, congestion and similar respiratory problems, and flatulence.
Household A popular ingredient of pot-pourri.

Propagation Take semi-ripe cuttings in summer; divide in early spring or autumn.
Growing Cut down all top growth to just above soil level in mid- to late autumn. Mulch lightly in spring and autumn, and give a balanced, general organic fertilizer, such as seaweed, in spring.
Harvesting Pick fresh leaves during the summer; cut leaves and flowers for drying just when the flowers are fully open.

▼ *Monarda citriodora*

▼ *Monarda* 'Beauty of Cobham' AGM

▼ *Monarda didyma*

▼ *Monarda fistulosa*

Myrrhis odorata

Sweet Cicely or myrrh

Description

FRESH, LIGHT green, ferny foliage is accompanied in spring by small umbels of white flowers. The leaves are amongst the earliest growths to thrust upwards from the bare soil of the herb garden in early spring. Sweet Cicely (and don't ask me who Cicely was) has the advantage over many members of the family (which include caraway, chervil, coriander, dill and yarrow) in that it grows to just a modest height – some 3ft (1m) or so after two or three years. This genus, despite its common name of myrrh, is not the same plant as the Biblical myrrh.

Recommended varieties

THE NORMAL species is likely to be the only one that you see.

▽ **Myrrhis odorata**

Known uses

Ornamental appeal Pretty enough, but best kept to the herb garden really.
Culinary Chop leaves finely and use in soups, stews, salad dressings and omelettes. Add leaves to the pot when cooking cabbage. Cook with gooseberries, currants and rhubarb to reduce acidity. Add unripe seeds (which have a sweet, nutty flavour) to fruit salads, apple pie and ice cream. The root can be cooked as a vegetable, or peeled raw and chopped for adding to salads.
Cosmetic None.
Medicinal Leaves make a useful 'sweetener', especially for diabetics. Infuse pieces of root and use as a tonic; at one time, boiled root was prescribed for the elderly.
Household Crushed seed can be used as a furniture polish.

How to grow

USDA zone Z4
Site Light shade.
Soil Rich, moist, but fairly free-draining soil.
Propagation Sow fresh seed in the garden in autumn; packeted seed can be difficult to germinate. Sweet Cicely self-seeds readily. Divide clumps in autumn or spring.
Growing Apply a balanced, organic, general fertilizer in spring, followed by a mulch, and mulch again in the autumn. Cut back all above-ground growth to soil level as soon as the leaves die down in late autumn.
Harvesting Cut young leaves and stems as required, from early spring to early autumn; they do not dry well.

Myrtus communis AGM
Myrtle

Description

MYRTLE IS one of the most exquisitely aromatic plants you will come across, and it is worthy of a place in the garden purely on ornamental grounds. Masses of small, dark, evergreen leaves are accompanied by beautiful, small, pure white flowers with golden stamens in summer. It is not the hardiest of subjects, however, and it really only does well in warm, sheltered gardens. In such places it can make a wonderful hedge, but it does have valuable and ancient herbal uses as well.

Recommended varieties

THE COMMON myrtle (*Myrtus communis* AGM) is the most frequently grown, but there are several named forms, including 'Variegata' (dark green and silver leaves, with flowers of a pinkish hue) and *Myrtus communis* subsp. *tarentina* AGM, known as the tarentina myrtle (small, oval, dark green leaves).

▼ **Myrtus communis AGM**

▼ **Myrtus communis subsp. *tarentina* AGM**

Known uses

Ornamental appeal As well as being ideal for the herb garden, myrtle is good in the shrub or mixed border, as a specimen shrub in a patio container, or as a low hedge.

Culinary Dried and powdered buds, and berries, can be used as a spice. Stuff leaves inside roast pork for a delicate flavour. Small branches (such as prunings) can be laid under roast pork for the last 10 minutes of cooking, or on barbecues when grilling lamb.

Cosmetic Decoct the berries to make a rinse to use on dark hair.

Medicinal Infuse leaves to make a powerful antiseptic and astringent; use as a tea for sinusitis. Apply in a compress to bruises.

Household Every part of the herb can be dried for use in pot-pourri. Add a decoction to furniture polish.

How to grow

USDA zone Z7–9
Site Full sun, on a site protected from the wind.
Soil Any well-drained soil.
  Propagation Take semi-ripe cuttings in mid- or late summer.
  Growing Clip back overgrown plants in late spring (after flowering), otherwise no pruning is necessary. Apply a balanced, organic, high-potash fertilizer in mid-spring, followed by a mulch, and mulch again in the autumn.
Harvesting Pick buds, flowers and ripe berries as they become available. The sweetest-scented leaves are to be had when the plant is in flower.

Nepeta racemosa AGM
Catmint, catnip or dog mint

Description

THIS PLANT is unrivalled for its long succession of lavender-blue flowers and for its almost magnetic-like attraction for cats (who are soon put off if a thorny twig is threaded into the plant – well, it is better than having the plant ruined). It grows to some 18in (45cm) in height and flowers all summer long. Catmint (which is in the same plant family as mint, but a different genus) has coarsely toothed, heart-shaped, grey-green leaves, and they have a penetrating mint-like scent. The flowers are some of the best in the garden for attracting bees and butterflies.

Recommended varieties

THERE ARE many species of *Nepeta*, and they are mainly grown in the ornamental garden. There are two species both labelled 'catmint': *Nepeta racemosa* AGM and *N. cataria*. Both have the same herbal and garden uses, but the former can be grown with some success in a pot on the windowsill. *N. racemosa* has more rounded leaves, whilst *N. cataria* has more pointed leaves.

▼ **Nepeta racemosa AGM**

Known uses

Ornamental appeal *N. racemosa* makes an attractive edging plant; otherwise catmints are best placed in the herb garden
Culinary Rub leaves on meat to give a mint-like flavour. Young, soft shoots can be added to spring and summer salads.
Cosmetic None.
Medicinal The leaves are high in vitamin C, therefore infusions of the leaves are used to relieve colds and fevers. Also used to treat headaches, stomach upsets and colic in children. It is also a mild sedative.
Household Dry and stuff leaves and shoots into cloth bags as 'toys' for cats. The scent of catmint is known to repel rats.

How to grow

USDA zone Z4
Site Sun or light shade.
Soil Any, as long as it is free-draining.
Propagation Sow seed in spring. Take any softwood cuttings in late spring. Lift and divide plants in spring.
Growing Cut plants back in autumn and mulch. Give a balanced, general organic fertilizer in spring. The fragrance released by cutting or bruising the plant will attract cats, who then molest the plant. Therefore plants grown from seed in situ are less likely to be 'attacked' than transplanted plants; the latter may need protecting in some way.
Harvesting Pick leaves when young and when flowering stops.

Ocimum basilicum
Basil or **sweet basil**

Description

BASIL IS an attractive, branching herb with large, juicy, oval, green leaves, possessing a spicy aroma: it is a good culinary companion to tomatoes. Tiny, insignificant, white or pinkish flowers are produced in summer. Basil is not hardy, but can be kept indoors on a windowsill during winter. Fewer gardeners are growing basil these days, in the main because supermarkets sell small pots of it, and therefore it is available cheaply and conveniently. An organic gardener may take the view – which I subscribe to – that, as basil is so easy and cheap to grow from seed, it is better still to grow it from scratch oneself. And this will cut back on plant miles, too.

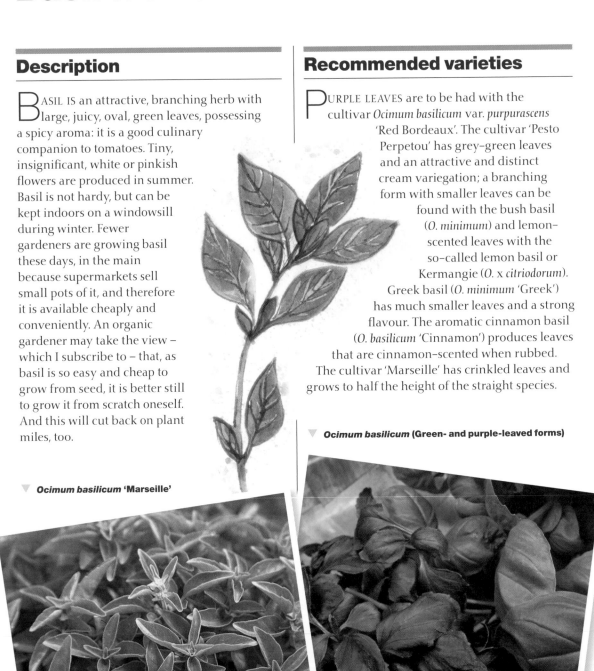

▼ *Ocimum basilicum* '**Marseille**'

Recommended varieties

PURPLE LEAVES are to be had with the cultivar *Ocimum basilicum* var. *purpurascens* 'Red Bordeaux'. The cultivar 'Pesto Perpetou' has grey–green leaves and an attractive and distinct cream variegation; a branching form with smaller leaves can be found with the bush basil (*O. minimum*) and lemon-scented leaves with the so-called lemon basil or Kermangie (*O.* x *citriodorum*). Greek basil (*O. minimum* 'Greek') has much smaller leaves and a strong flavour. The aromatic cinnamon basil (*O. basilicum* 'Cinnamon') produces leaves that are cinnamon–scented when rubbed. The cultivar 'Marseille' has crinkled leaves and grows to half the height of the straight species.

▼ *Ocimum basilicum* (Green- and purple-leaved forms)

How to grow

USDA zone Z4–9
Site Full sun.
Soil Basil prefers a slightly acidic soil.
Propagation It is best to start new plants each year. Sow as an annual in early spring, preferably in a propagator with some bottom heat. After the danger of frost has passed, sow outdoors in situ, or in pots.
Growing Syringe (finely spray) leaves with clean tap water in hot weather; a fine mist should be the aim rather than large droplets of water, to avoid the risk of leaf scorch. Occasional summer clipping will keep the plants neat.
Harvesting Pick leaves when needed; they are far better when young. Harvest the tops when the flowers open.

▽ *Ocimum basilicum* '**Pesto Perpetou**'

Known uses

Ornamental appeal Grow in the herb garden, or in a container outdoors for the summer (keep near to the back door for convenience).
Culinary Add leaves to salads and sandwiches; they are the ideal accompaniment to tomatoes and/or garlic. Used in pesto sauce for many Mediterranean dishes. Pound leaves with oil, or tear them with fingers, rather than chop.
Cosmetic Add an infusion of the flowering tops and leaves for an invigorating bath.
Medicinal Infuse leaves as a tea to aid digestion. A few drops of essential oil on a sleeve (to be inhaled) can allay mental fatigue.
Household Pots on windowsills will deter flies.

▽ *Ocimum minimum* '**Greek**'

Origanum
Oregano, marjoram

Description

OFTEN CALLED marjoram, this has a variety of flavouring uses – in salads, stuffings, and with cooked meat (chicken especially), fish, eggs and cheese; it's worth experimenting with. Common oregano (*Origanum vulgare*; Z4) is a slightly sprawling plant with dark green, peppery-flavoured leaves. There are variegated and golden-leaved forms. The small white or purple flowers, which are produced in summer, are highly attractive to bees and butterflies.

Recommended varieties

SWEET MARJORAM (*O. majorana*; Z10) is a tender form that needs winter protection. The pot or French marjoram (*O. onites*; Z8) has mid-green, savoury-flavoured leaves and white or pink flowers. *O. rotundifolium* AGM (Z8) produces hanging funnel-shaped flowers in summer in clusters surrounded by yellowish green bracts. *O. vulgare* 'Aureum' AGM has leaves of an all-over bright gold, whilst 'Gold Tip' has green leaves with bright golden tips, and 'Country Cream' has an unobtrusive variegation of cream to the edges of the leaves. One of the best for flowers is *O. laevigatum* 'Herrenhausen' AGM, with bright pink-mauve blooms in summer.

Origanum vulgare

Origanum vulgare 'Aureum' AGM

Origanum vulgare 'Gold Tip'

How to grow

USDA zone Z4–10
Site Full sun is best, but plants will tolerate light shade; note that the golden–leaved forms will scorch in full sun.
Soil It prefers a slightly alkaline soil, but this should be fertile and well drained.
Propagation Take semi–ripe cuttings in late summer. The most attractive or versatile forms do not come true from seed; only the species types will do this.
Growing Give plants a light dressing of general organic fertilizer in spring. Cut plants hard back to soil level in autumn; or leave the seed heads in place to provide bird food during winter. Renew plants every three or four years. These plants can be grown in pots on the windowsill, but they will need replacing every year to keep them small and manageable.
Harvesting Pick young leaves at any stage of the growing year. If you intend to preserve the leaves, they are best picked just before the flowers open.

Known uses

Ornamental appeal Most of the more ornate marjorams (basically any other than straight *O. vulgare*) could usefully be grown in patio containers or as plants towards the front of a flower border.
Culinary The leaves of sweet marjoram can be chopped finely for salads and butter sauces for fish, and can be infused as an aromatic tea. The leaves of common and French oregano can be added to egg, tomato, cheese and pasta dishes, and pizza. Often included in bouquet garni.
Cosmetic Make a strong infusion to be used as a hair conditioner.
Medicinal Chew leaves, or rub on a drop of essential oil for temporary relief of toothache. Infuse flowering tops of sweet marjoram as a tea for colds, headaches and nervous disorders. Make a compress of leaves and flowering tops for relief from rheumatic pains and tension.
Household Add pulverized leaves or a strong decoction to furniture polish.

▼ *Origanum* '**Country Cream**'   ▼ *Origanum rotundifolium* **AGM**   ▼ *Origanum laevigatum* '**Herrenhausen**' **AGM**

Papaver
Poppy

Description

THE POPPY is familiar to gardeners as a decorative border plant (mainly forms of *Papaver orientalis*), and it has also become the symbol of remembrance (following usage of the field or Flanders' poppy, *P. rhoeas*). Various species also give us oil, edible seed and (in the case of *P. somniferum*) opium, which is the source of morphine and codeine as well as heroin.

Recommended varieties

THERE ARE a great many cultivars available to the ornamental gardener, but to the herb gardener the last two mentioned above are the most important. One of the most ornamental is *P. somniferum* var. *paeoniiflorum*, a form of the opium poppy, with very double, peony–like flowers in pink, red, purple or white.

▼ **Papaver somniferum**

Known uses

Ornamental appeal Good for the flower garden. Dried seed heads are good for indoor decoration.
Culinary Sprinkle seeds on breads and cakes to provide a nutty flavour.
Cosmetic None.
Medicinal Seeds from the opium poppy exude a latex that has been used to relieve pain and diarrhoea, but tend now to be used as the main source of the painkiller morphine. All parts of the opium poppy, except the ripe seed, are dangerous. Only qualified medical practitioners should use them medicinally.
Household None.

How to grow

USDA zone Z5–7
Site Full sun.
Soil Any soil as long as it is well drained.
Propagation Sow in spring or autumn, in situ. Field poppies need a period of cold in order for germination to be triggered.
Growing Poppies have a tendency occasionally to collapse and die when in full growth. This is sometimes, but not always, due to the presence of red ants, who love to make their nests among the thong–like roots.
Harvesting Collect seed when the capsule is ripe.

Pelargonium
Scented geranium

Description

Unlike the hardy geranium or cranesbill, pelargoniums have relatively small, unscented flowers, but the fragrant leaves are present all year round. They can be used in small quantities to add flavour to puddings, and can be used as natural air fresheners. Simply by brushing past a plant or rubbing the leaves between your fingers, you can release wonderful, sometimes spicy, sometimes fruity, fragrances. All pelargoniums are half–hardy, evergreen perennials, best grown in pots or in the conservatory.

Recommended varieties

There are dozens of species and hybrids that have the scented properties beloved of herbalists. Some of the best species include are the rose–scented pelargonium (*Pelargonium capitatum*) with velvety, crinkled, rose–scented leaves; *P. citronellum* with deeply veined, strongly lemon–scented leaves; *P. dichondrifolium* with white flowers and leaves that are strongly scented of lavender; and the delightful lemon pelargonium (*P. crispum*) with crinkled, kidney–shaped leaves and a strong lemon fragrance.

▽ ***Pelargonium* 'Madame Salleron' AGM**
　　　　　　　　　▽ ***Pelargonium dichondrifolium***

Known uses

Ornamental appeal Good pot plants for conservatories and summer patio plants.
Culinary Rose-scented varieties can flavour stewed apples and pears, and jellies. Infuse leaves in milk, cream and syrups.
Cosmetic The oil is used in perfumery and skin-care products.
Medicinal Can be used externally as a poultice for bruises and sprains, and as a rub for aching feet or legs.
Household Add dried leaves to pot-pourri, or to muslin bags to scent clothes.

As for cultivars, look for 'Lady Plymouth' AGM (small, pink flowers with deeply cut, small, grey–green and cream variegated leaves), 'Madame Salleron' AGM (a non–flowering cultivar with variegated green and white leaves) and 'Chocolate Peppermint' (clusters of very small, white–pink flowers in summer, with green and brown variegated leaves that smell of peppermint and a hint of chocolate).

How to grow

Zone Z10
Site Full sun.
Soil Well drained; best in containers with a loam–based compost.
Propagation Sow seed in spring. Take stem cuttings of new growth in early summer.
Growing Water in dry weather, but do not let plants sit with their roots in water. Nip out the growing tips to keep plants bushy.
Harvesting Pick leaves to use fresh, or for drying, in early summer.

Petroselinum crispum
Parsley

Description

ALONG WITH lavender and various forms of mint, parsley is one of the herbs most often grown by amateur gardeners. The ancient Greeks associated it with death so avoided it, but the Romans used it to disguise strong odours. It is said (originally by the Romans) that parsley seed has 'to go to the devil and back seven times' before it will germinate. This is alluding to the fact that it resides in the soil a long time.

Recommended varieties

THERE ARE three main types of parsley (all *Petroselinum crispum*), although only the first two are considered herbs (the third is more a vegetable). The traditional curly-leaved parsley is *P. crispum*. Look for 'Bravour' AGM (strong stems and tightly curled leaves) and 'Super Moss Curled' (dwarf, compact and ideal for pots). *P. crispum* var. *neapolitanum* is the French or Italian parsley with larger, flattened leaves. *P. crispum* var. *tuberosum* is the Hamburg or turnip-rooted, grown as a root vegetable (like parsnip) for its flavour that's a cross between parsley and celery.

How to grow

Zone Z5
Site Sun or partial shade.
Soil Rich, well-drained, neutral to alkaline soil.
Propagation Sow seed from spring to late summer; germination takes three to six weeks. It can help to soak seeds overnight in warm water.
Growing Winter crops will probably need protection in frost-prone areas.
Harvesting Leaves are picked – before flowering – and used fresh, frozen, juiced or dried. Roots are harvested in late autumn. Seeds are collected when ripe.

▼ *Petroselinum crispum* 'Bravour' AGM

Known uses

Ornamental appeal An attractive edging to the kitchen garden or foliage plants in pots.
Culinary Leaves are a fresh garnish to many kinds of cooked dishes. Also used to flavour sauces, butter, dressings and stuffings.
Cosmetic Oil is used in perfumes for men.
Medicinal Leaves are strongly diuretic. A hair rinse made from the seeds is effective for killing head lice. Do not take medically when pregnant.
Household None.

Rosa
Rose

Description

THE ROSE is not generally thought of as a herb but it does have very many herbal uses – and when planted in a herb garden does appear to be in perfect harmony with its neighbours. Shrub roses are especially suited to the herb grower, but the modern hybrid tea and floribunda cultivars may still be harvested for their herbal qualities.

Recommended varieties

THE OLD rose known as Rosamundi (*Rosa gallica* 'Versicolor') has striking pale pink, dark pink and magenta stripes on the petals. The apothecary's rose, also known as the red rose of Lancaster (*R. gallica* 'Officinalis'), is an all-over deep pink. The damask rose (*R. damascena*) is rose–pink, highly scented and semi–double (this species is the source of rose oil and rose water). The eglantine or sweet briar (*R. eglanteria*, formerly *R. rubiginosa*) has small, pink, fragrant single flowers with apple–scented leaves. The wild or dog rose (*R. canina*) has strong, arching, prickly stems, with pink or white fragrant flowers and bright red autumn hips.

Rosa gallica 'Officinalis'   **Rosa eglanteria**

Known uses

Ornamental appeal Shrub roses have mass appeal, and are best grown in a shrub or mixed border, or as a specimen plant in a lawn or a large patio container.

Culinary Sprinkle petals into salads, or into fruit pies. They can also be used in desserts, syrups and sorbets. Rose water can be used to flavour sweets and drinks. Pureed hips (with the external hairs removed) can be used in teas, wine, syrups and jams.

Cosmetic Use rose oil as a perfume, and use rosewater as an antiseptic tonic to soothe inflamed skin.

Medicinal Make a tea or syrup of the hips, which are high in vitamins B, C, E and K.

Household Add petals to pot-pourri.

How to grow

USDA zone Z5–7

Site Sunny and open, but not too exposed.

Soil In general, roses prefer a slightly alkaline soil.

Propagation Sow seed of species roses, or take cuttings in autumn.

Growing Prune shrub roses lightly in early spring. Feed with an organic seaweed fertilizer monthly during the growing season. Deadhead as required.

Harvesting Cut rose buds when they have formed. Petals are best harvested just after they have opened. Pick hips when ripe.

Rosmarinus officinalis

Rosemary

Description

ROSEMARY, CLASSED as a 'woody herb', is grown for its aromatic foliage, with sprigs used for flavouring and scenting various meat and fish dishes. It makes a fine and decorative garden plant, however. *Rosmarinus officinalis* is the usual species grown. It reaches around 5ft (1.5m) in height, and has narrow, grey–green leaves and clusters of small, pale blue flowers in spring and early summer. Rosemary was well known in ancient Greece and Rome, and it gained an early reputation for improving memory and uplifting the spirits. It is native to the Mediterranean coastline, and is found on sunny hillsides and in open situations. Although *R. officinalis* is frost–hardy, not all species are.

Recommended varieties

MORE UPRIGHT, or fastigiated in habit is 'Miss Jessop's Upright' AGM. The prostrate form, 'McConnell's Blue' AGM, can be used on a rockery, and is good grown in a patio container where it can tumble over the sides. 'Primley Blue' (not 'Frimley Blue', which has been misapplied for some years) is aromatic and a good, hardy variety with dark green leaves. *R. officinalis* var. *angustissimus* 'Bennenden Blue' AGM has flowers of a darker blue than most, and the white rosemary (*R. officinalis* var. *albiflorus*) is slightly shorter than the main species; it reaches just 32in (80cm) or so in height. 'Aureus', meanwhile, has thin needle–like leaves that are splashed with gold. It hardly ever flowers, but when it does they are very pale blue.

▼ **Rosmarinus officinalis**

▼ **Rosmarinus officinalis 'Miss Jessop's Upright' AGM**

How to grow

USDA zone Z8
Site Some shelter from prevailing winds is desirable, along with a sunny location.
Soil Any dryish soil.
Propagation Sow seeds in spring. Take semi-ripe cuttings and place in a soil–based compost during late summer.
Growing Mulch and feed in spring with a general organic fertilizer. Mulch again in autumn if your soil is sandy and 'hungry'. Prune by cutting out the oldest third of the branches every spring; rosemary may be clipped to shape with the inevitable loss of some flowers. If rosemary is planted near to carrots it is reputed to repel carrot fly, and it is also believed that when planted near to sage, there is a mutual benefit to both plants.
Harvesting As rosemary is evergreen, you can pick the leaves, or sprigs, all year round.

▽ *Rosmarinus officinalis* **'Primley Blue'**

Known uses

Ornamental appeal A good plant for a mixed or shrub border, or patio container. A must for the herb garden.
Culinary Rosemary is indispensable in the kitchen; sprigs have been used traditionally to garnish roasted lamb, but it is also good with other meats (especially pork). Chop leaves and flowers to use in salads, herb butters and to flavour baked potatoes.
Cosmetic Leaves make a good rinse for dark hair. They can also be used to make a facial steam bath, and are said to stimulate blood circulation when added to a bath.
Medicinal Can be used as an antiseptic gargle and mouthwash.
Household Boil a handful of rosemary for 10 minutes or so in 16fl oz (475ml) of water, to make an antiseptic solution for washing bathroom fittings.

Rumex acetosa

Sorrel

Description

THE COMMON or garden sorrel (*Rumex acetosa*) is sometimes called the broad leaf sorrel. It is a hardy herbaceous perennial with broad, lance–shaped, bright green leaves and upright growth reaching a height of some 30in (75cm). The leaves are almost tasteless early in the season; acidity develops as the season progresses. The flowers appear on tall, reddish–green spikes in summer.

Recommended varieties

BUCKLER–LEAVED SORREL (*Rumex scutatus*) has small, light green leaves with silvery patches on them, and grows to around 18in (45cm). It is sometimes referred to as French sorrel. There are weed forms, too.

▼ *Rumex acetosa*

How to grow

USDA zone Z3–6
Site Sun or partial shade.
Soil A rich, moist soil.

Propagation Sow seed in the garden or in pots in mid– to late spring. Divide clumps in early spring or autumn.

Growing Sorrel can be grown in pots if clipped and well fed, but comparatively little foliage is produced. Any tall flower spikes should be removed to encourage leafy growth.

Harvesting Sorrel does not dry well, so pick young leaves for using fresh; they can be frozen throughout the growing season.

Known uses

Ornamental appeal This looks like a weed, and to many people it is. Confine it to a patch in the herb garden.
Culinary Add leaves to salads, or use to make a soup. Cook like spinach (but change the cooking water once to reduce acidity).
Cosmetic None.
Medicinal Infuse as a tea to treat liver and kidney ailments. Apply leaves to infected wounds, boils and mouth ulcers.
Household The juice of sorrel is effective in bleaching mould, ink and rust stains from cloth, wicker and silver.

Ruta graveolens

Rue

Description

RUE WAS the first herb I grew professionally, and I have always loved it, from its small, rounded blue–grey leaves to its greenish–yellow, frilled flowers in late summer. Plants can grow to 30in (75cm) or so after a couple of years. Many people vehemently dislike rue because of the powerful pungency that comes from a mass of oil glands dotted over the leaves. I maintain they smell strongly of coconut, whilst others have likened the aroma to cat's urine. The leaves are believed to be the inspiration for the design of the suit of clubs in packs of playing cards.

Recommended varieties

RUTA GRAVEOLENS 'Variegata' has leaves of pale green with splashes of bright cream. This plant often produces stems that revert to all–green; simply cut these off at their base, and leave the variegated foliage alone. *R. graveolens* 'Jackman's Blue' is a more compact plant, with metallic blue leaves.

▼ **Ruta graveolens**

▼ **Ruta graveolens 'Variegata'**

Known uses

Ornamental appeal Plants are seen at their best on their own, rather than in a mixed border.
Culinary The leaves are bitter-tasting, but very small amounts can give an interesting muskiness to egg, fish and cream-cheese dishes. Traditionally, seed was used (with lovage and mint) as a marinade for partridge. Use with caution.
Cosmetic Infuse leaves to bathe tired eyes.
Medicinal Infused as a tea, the leaves are often used to treat wounds and various blood-related conditions. However, rue should only be used under expert supervision, for the leaves also have insecticidal properties. They can be particularly dangerous for pregnant women.
Household None.

How to grow

USDA zone Z5
Site Full sun to light shade.
Soil Well drained and preferably alkaline. A poor to moderately fertile soil seems to produce hardier plants.
   Propagation Sow species only in spring (rue is slow to germinate). Also, you can divide in spring and take stem cuttings in late summer.
   Growing Outdoor plants should be given some winter protection, especially if you live in a cold area or your garden is exposed. Cut plants back in spring to keep them tidy.
Harvesting Pick young leaves; they are at their best just before the late–summer flowers open. Collect seeds when available.

Salvia officinalis

Sage

Description

I T IS becoming more common to see the herb sage (*Salvia officinalis*), and its purple–leaved version, used as bedding. It makes useful decorative foliage for the front of borders, and can of course be grown in permanent planting situations. It is also a tactile (with soft, felted leaves) and aromatic plant, so is regularly grown in sensory gardens. An evergreen, highly aromatic, shrubby perennial, sage grows to 2ft (60cm) or so. It has downy, textured, grey–green leaves and spikes of violet–blue flowers in early summer. There are some 900 species of the *Salvia* genus worldwide, and this is the most commonly found of the herb types.

Recommended varieties

T HE STRIKING purple sage (*Salvia officinalis* 'Purpurascens' AGM) has purple, grey and green foliage. *S. officinalis* 'Variegata' has light green and dark green variegations. The tricolor sage (*S. officinalis* 'Tricolor') has leaves of green, cream and purple, and to some people is too garish for a place in the ornamental garden. The pineapple sage (*S. elegans*) is a tender perennial with green, soft leaves that have a pineapple scent. It also produces tubular, scarlet flowers in winter (but for this it will need protection under cover). There is only one true annual – *S. viridis* (formerly *S. horminum*) that has historically been used as a culinary herb. It is more frequently grown as an ornamental plant for its coloured bracts, which crown the flowering stems. For years just the species was available, but recently we have seen the introduction of the Marble Arch Series, which has given us blue, white and rose

▼ *Salvia officinalis* 'Purpurascens' AGM   ▼ *Salvia officinalis* 'Tricolor'   ▼ *Salvia elegans*

options. Another excellent plant is clary sage (*S. sclarea*), a biennial. It has large, wrinkled leaves and long-lasting, lilac flowers.

How to grow

USDA zone Z5
Site A warm dry soil, preferably in full sun.
Soil A free-draining soil, either neutral or slightly alkaline.
Propagation Sow seed of species (and annual) types in spring; germination usually takes two to three weeks. Take softwood cuttings of all bar the annual types in late spring or early summer. If you have a well-established sage, or if it is becoming woody, layer established branches in spring or autumn.
Growing Maintain compact plants with plenty of young growth by cutting plants back in spring; this will reduce the amount of flowering but improve leaf performance. Neaten plants after flowering by giving a light trim. In autumn protect all half-hardy sages and first-year plants.

Known uses

Ornamental appeal Most sages make useful border plants for the ornamental garden. They are not really suited to growing in patio containers.
Culinary Leaves are used to flavour Mediterranean dishes, cheese, sausages, pork and other fatty meats. Traditionally sage is also made into stuffings (a classic combination being sage and onion). Leaves of pineapple sage may be floated in drinks.
Cosmetic An infusion of the leaves makes a rinse for dark hair and to treat dandruff.
Medicinal Infusions are taken internally as tonics and to aid digestion. Use also as a gargle or mouthwash for sore throats, mouth ulcers, laryngitis, tonsillitis and gum disease.
Household Dried leaves, especially those of pineapple sage, work well in pot-pourri.

Harvesting Pick fresh leaves as required and when available; although technically evergreen, sage leaves are frequently old, gnarled and crispy in winter. Leaves can be dried, but they taste nothing like the fresh version.

▼ *Salvia officinalis 'Variegata'*

▼ *Salvia sclarea*

Sambucus nigra

Elder

Description

A DECIDUOUS SHRUB or small tree, the elder is a common sight in old–style hedgerows, where its cream–white flowers in late spring are picked to make elderflower water (reputed to be good for the complexion) and the highly palatable and fragrant elderflower 'champagne'. The attractive golden, purple and cut–leaf forms are useful in large, informal herb gardens. The most eagerly awaited attribute, however, is probably the autumn berries, rich in vitamin C, that are picked for making jams, cordials and wine. This is not so much a plant to grow and nurture, as a wild plant with attributes that we can make use of.

Recommended varieties

THE SPECIES *Sambucus nigra* is usually grown for its herbal qualities, but there are more attractive forms available in 'Aurea' AGM (with golden leaves) and 'Marginata' (with cream variegations to the leaves).

How to grow

USDA zone Z5
Site Full sun or part shade.
Soil It prefers a slightly alkaline soil.
Propagation The elder readily self–seeds. Or take semi–ripe cuttings in late summer.
Growing Prune to keep in shape between mid–autumn and mid–spring.
Harvesting Pick leaves at any time during the growing season. Harvest the fresh flowers and berries when available.

Known uses

Ornamental appeal Mainly a shrub for the hedgerow or boundary. Various golden and variegated forms are available.
Culinary Use the berries to make jams and use both the fresh flowers and berries to make wine, vinegars and to flavour tarts.
Cosmetic Elderflower water whitens and softens the skin, and many maintain it is effective at removing freckles.
Medicinal A gargle made from elderflower infusion relieves sore throats and tonsillitis. Elderflowers and berries are mildly laxative. A cold infusion of the flowers may be used as an eye wash for conjunctivitis.
Household Dry the leaves to use in insect-repellent sachets. The wood from the adult plant is highly prized by craftsmen. The berries make a lavender or violet dye when combined with alum (one of several mineral substances usually available from the chemist, or from health-food or even grocery stores that stock spices).

▼ *Sambucus nigra* **'Marginata'**

Sanguisorba minor
Salad burnet

Description

THIS IS a hardy perennial that keeps green foliage throughout the winter. It reaches a height of just 12in (30cm), but retains a tight, compact habit. The leaves are composed of finely toothed leaflets. The early to mid–summer flowers comprise tiny green blooms, with red points, packed into spherical heads just ½in (1cm) or so across.

Recommended varieties

A LARGER VERSION is available in the form of the great burnet (*Sanguisorba officinalis*). It grows to about 4ft (1.2m) in height.

How to grow

USDA zone Z4–5
Site Sun or partial shade.
Soil Salad burnet is a native of chalk downlands, so in a garden situation it is best planted in a limey, well–drained soil.
Propagation Sow seed in the garden, or in pots, in mid– to late spring, or in late summer. It germinates readily, and established plants sometimes self–seed.
Growing Cut back the flowering stems and old leaves regularly to produce plenty of new, tender young leaves.
Harvesting Pick leaves for using fresh all year round. The leaves do not dry well.

Known uses

Ornamental appeal This plant does not have a particularly strong aesthetic appeal, so keep it in the herb garden, or in a pot near to the back door for easy access.
Culinary The leaves have a mild cucumber flavour and are useful in salads and as a garnish, particularly in winter. They can be floated in drink or wine punch. Put chopped leaves into a herb vinegar.
Cosmetic Infuse leaves to make a facial wash for sore skin and sunburn.
Medicinal Leaves on food are thought to aid digestion.
Household Press dried leaves into the sides of slightly melted candles, for a pleasing fragrance.

Sanguisorba minor

Santolina
Cotton lavender

Description

EVEN WHEN not in flower, the tight, silver–grey, very finely divided leaves make santolinas worth growing. The flowers are in small, button–like heads carried above the foliage on long stalks in mid– to late summer. Santolinas make small, evergreen shrubs and can be trimmed into mini–hedges.

Recommended varieties

THE FORM that is most widely seen in gardens is *Santolina chamaecyparissus* AGM, with silver, cypress–like foliage and bright yellow flowers. *S. pinnata* subsp. *neapolitana* AGM has lemon–yellow flowers, whilst a cultivar of it – 'Sulphurea' – has flowers of a warmer yellow. *S. rosmarinifolia* has small, rosemary–like, willow–green leaves, which are slightly less aromatic than the others. *S. viridis* has thread–like, pungent, vivid green leaves and yellow, button flowers in summer.

▼ *Santolina chamaecyparissus* AGM

▼ *Santolina pinnata* subsp. *neapolitana* AGM

How to grow

USDA zone Z7
Site Full sun.
Soil Any well–drained to dry soil.
Propagation Sow seed of species in spring and summer. Take cuttings of any form in spring, or from mid–summer to autumn (but these will need to be given winter protection).
Growing Clip to shape (whether grown as individual plants or as low hedging) in spring or summer – but not in the autumn as new resultant growth will be too tender to come through winter unscathed. Deadhead plants in autumn.
Harvesting Pick leaves any time; harvest flowering stems in late summer.

Known uses

Ornamental appeal Good for the ornamental garden and patio containers. Can be grown as an effective, low, silver hedge (such as for path edging or knot gardens). Flowers can be dried for use in indoor arrangements.
Culinary None.
Cosmetic None.
Medicinal Santolina has several medicinal uses, ranging from the alleviation of jaundice to a treatment for internal parasites.
Household Small branches can be hung amongst clothes or laid in drawers to deter moths and other insects. Add leaves to pot-pourri.

Satureja
Savory

Description

THERE ARE essentially two types of savory – summer (*Satureja hortensis*) and winter (*S. montana*). Summer savory is a small, bushy, hardy annual growing to about 15in (38cm). It has woody, much-branched stems and small, leathery, dark green leaves. Tiny, white or pale lilac flowers appear in summer. With its spicy leaves, it is one of the oldest flavouring herbs, and it has been widely used over the centuries for its antiseptic and digestive properties. Winter savory is a semi-evergreen, clump-forming perennial. It contains a higher proportion of thymol in its leaves than summer savory, so it has a stronger, coarser fragrance.

Recommended varieties

SATUREJA SPICIGERA is the creeping winter savory, best grown on a rockery; its strongly flavoured, deep green leaves are sprinkled in late summer with tiny, white flowers.

▼ **Satureja montana**   ▼ **Satureja hortensis**

How to grow

USDA zone Z6
Site Full sun.
Soil Well-drained and preferably a poor, alkaline soil.
Propagation Sow seed in containers, or in situ, in early spring. Winter savory can also be propagated by division in spring and by cuttings in summer.
Growing Keep picking summer savory and do not allow it to flower if you want to maintain its flavour. Protect it from the freezing conditions in autumn and winter.
Harvesting Pick leaves just as flower buds are formed. Collect flowering tops in late summer.

Known uses

Ornamental appeal Winter savory can make a good edging plant, otherwise keep the savories to the herb garden or patio pots.
Culinary Summer savory has an affinity with beans, and adds a spicy flavour to pulses, dried herb mixtures, stuffings, pâtés and meat dishes. Winter savory is used similarly, but to most tastes it has a less refined flavour.
Cosmetic Use the flowering tops as an antiseptic in facial steam baths for oily skin.
Medicinal Summer savory has antiseptic, antibacterial properties and is said to improve digestion. The savories stimulate the uterus and pregnant women must not be given them in medicinal doses, unless under qualified medical supervision.
Household Throw stems and leaves onto fires to make an aromatic disinfectant.

Scutellaria galericulata
Skullcap

Description

THIS HARDY perennial is yet another member of the lavender and sage family. It reaches up to 2ft (60cm) or so in height. Branching stems carry oval, toothed leaves and small, pretty blue flowers appear along the stem during summer. The roots are fibrous and yellow.

Recommended varieties

ALTHOUGH THIS is quite a large genus, only *Scutellaria galericulata* and the Virginian skullcap (*S. lateriflora*) – which is almost identical but slightly larger – are commonly grown for their herbal properties.

▼ *Scutellaria galericulata*

Known uses

Ornamental appeal Little real ornamental appeal, so best confined to the herb garden, or planted in a patio container.
Culinary None.
Cosmetic None.
Medicinal All parts of the plant are useful, but the flowers and leaves are most often used. Dry them, grind into a powder, and make into a tea. Skullcap is used in the treatment of anxiety, nervousness, hysteria, depression, insomnia and headaches.
Household None.

How to grow

USDA zone Z5
Site Full sun or light shade.
Soil Any soil as long as it is free–draining.
Propagation Sow seed under gentle heat in late winter. Divide roots in early spring. Take semi–ripe cuttings in summer.
Growing Mulch in autumn and spring, and give a balanced organic fertilizer in spring. Cut plants back to soil level in late autumn. Divide plants every three or four years.
Harvesting Pick the flowers and leaves (when available) for drying.

Symphytum officinale
Comfrey

Description

C OMFREY IS eagerly grown by organic gardeners for it is generally believed to contain more nutritional value as a fertilizer than any other member of the plant kingdom (see pages 24–25). The dark green leaves are oval, tapering to a point; they are rough and thick-ribbed. Flowers appear as blue-mauve bells in late spring.

Recommended varieties

S YMPHYTUM GRANDIFLORUM has creamy-red flowers, whilst *S. asperum* has flowers of bright blue. Russian comfrey (*Symphytum* x *uplandicum*) has more attractively pointed leaves. If your interest is in compost making then the selected 'Bocking' strains are better (these are usually only available from specialist organic gardening suppliers).

How to grow

USDA zone Z5
Site Full sun. A word of warning, however: choose your site carefully as comfrey roots are known to go down as far as 10ft (3m) and so plants are difficult to eradicate once established.
Soil A neutral soil is best, and preferably one rich in nitrogen.
Propagation Take root offsets (sections of root, each with a growing tip) any time of the year except mid-winter.
Growing For the best leaf growth, apply a bucketful of well-rotted animal manure around plants in spring and again in late summer.
Harvesting Pick leaves and stems in mid-summer. Lift roots in autumn and winter.

Known uses

Ornamental appeal This is more like a wild plant or weed than a bona-fide garden plant, and it can grow very well on waste ground. Therefore, confine it to a wild part of the garden, or to a dedicated area of the herb garden.
Culinary Leaves can be cooked like spinach, or chopped and added to salads. Blanch stems and cook like asparagus.
Cosmetic Infuse leaves and grated roots, and add to baths to soften skin.
Medicinal Fresh leaves can be stored for two years in an airtight container, and the exuded liquid 'oil' can be used externally to treat skin irritations.
Household None.

Warning: Comfrey is believed to cause liver damage if large quantities are consumed over a long period of time.

▼ ***Symphytum* x *uplandicum***

Tanacetum

Alecost, feverfew, pyrethrum, tansy

Description

THE *TANACETUM* genus is a significant member of the daisy family and, whilst not huge, has given us several, entirely different, important types of herb. Feverfew (*T. parthenium*) is arguably the most important, having received worldwide acclaim as a cure for headaches. The leaves are aromatic, yellowish–green and chrysanthemum–like. The white–petalled flowers are typically daisy–like. Tansy (*T. vulgare*) has thinner, fern–like leaves that are rich in potassium. Pyrethrum (*T. cinerarifolium*) is grown commercially for its insecticidal properties.

Recommended varieties

THE GOLDEN feverfew (*T. parthenium* 'Aureum') has deeply golden leaves. Curled tansy (*T. vulgare* var. *crispum*) carries leaves that are dark green, crinkly and curly. The cultivar 'Isla Gold' has golden variegated leaves, whilst 'Silver Lace' is green and silver. *T. coccineum* is an attractive garden plant with similar insecticidal properties to pyrethrum; it produces flower heads of white or red, sometimes tipped with yellow.

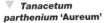
▼ *Tanacetum parthenium* 'Aureum'

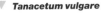
▼ *Tanacetum vulgare*

How to grow

USDA zone Z3–9
Site Full sun; tansy can tolerate light shade.
Soil Any that is well drained.
Propagation Sow seed in spring; feverfew self-seeds profusely. Divide roots in autumn.
Growing With the exception of feverfew, tanacetums are not generally suited to container-growing.
Harvesting Pick leaves and flowers any time they are available.

Known uses

Ornamental appeal Feverfew is an attractive plant and has as much of a place in the ornamental garden as it does in the herb plot.
Culinary Feverfew leaves, which taste bitter, can be added to food to 'cut' the grease. Stew tansy with rhubarb, and rub the leaves on meat as an alternative to rosemary.
Cosmetic The flowers and leaves of tansy are used in astringent baths and facial steams for mature, sallow and non-sensitive skins.
Medicinal Raw feverfew leaves in small doses can relieve migraines. The leaves are also a mild laxative. Also, infuse as a mouth rinse after tooth extraction. Use tansy externally as a compress to bring relief to painful rheumatic joints. Do not use tansy during pregnancy.
Household Use both feverfew and tansy leaves dried in sachets as a moth deterrent.

Thymus
Thyme

Description

THYME NEEDS little in the way of introduction as it must surely rank as one of the most often-grown four or five herbs. It is an ancient plant from the warm, sunny Mediterranean region. There are a great many species and cultivars, and between them they possess all the properties necessary for use in the ornamental garden, in the kitchen, on the make-up table, in the medicine cabinet and even in the cleaning cupboard. A member of the lavender family, thyme is generally a low-grower, often surprisingly tough, and it possesses thin, woody stems and small leaves, accompanied by tiny, fragrant flowers in shades of pink, red, lilac, mauve and white. Thymes vary from 2–15in (5–38cm) high.

Recommended varieties

THERE ARE many recommended varieties, and all are worthy plants for the herb garden, whilst many should be grown in the ornamental garden, too. *Thymus vulgaris* is the common thyme, with pale lilac blooms in early and mid-summer. The English wild thyme is *T. polytrichus* subsp. *britannicus*; it is probably the hardiest of thymes and is a creeping plant with mauve flowers. *T. pulegioides* 'Aureus' AGM and 'Bertram Anderson' AGM are both golden-yellow creeping thymes, whilst 'Archer's Gold' is more variegated; 'Foxley' is also variegated, with slightly larger leaves. *T. citriodorus* is lemon-scented and has pink flowers, whilst the excellent cultivar 'Doone Valley' is beautifully variegated with green, cream and yellow. *T.* Coccineus Group AGM is a creeper with crimson flowers and small, faintly scented leaves. *T.* 'Fragrantissimus' is a shrub with very pale lilac flowers and sweet, fruity, bluish-grey foliage. »

▼ *Thymus* Coccineus Group AGM

▼ *Thymus citriodorus*

▼ *Thymus* 'Fragrantissimus'

How to grow

USDA zone Z4–9
Site Full sun.
Soil The ideal soil is light, well–drained and moderately fertile; preferably neutral to slightly alkaline.
Propagation Take semi–ripe cuttings in late summer. This is best done every second year and the stock plants replaced by the new the following season. Thyme species may be raised from seed; the cultivars and hybrids will not come true from seed. The most effective and most attractive thymes are always propagated by cuttings, which are not difficult to strike.
Growing Little regular attention is required once plants are fully established. Lightly mulch plants in spring (and again in autumn if the soil is particularly thin and hungry), and give a little balanced organic fertilizer, such as seaweed, when the plant is in full growth in spring.
Harvesting Pick leaves in summer (they are at their best when the plant is flowering).

Known uses

Ornamental appeal Thyme, in its various colours, forms and styles, makes a good container plant (particularly as a component in a mixed herb pot). It can also be very effective when grown on a rock garden or at the front of (or an edging for) a mixed border.
Culinary Chopped leaves and flowers can be added to almost any savoury dish, but they go particularly well with cooked meats and in stuffings. Leaves and flowers can certainly be added to salads, but the texture of thyme can sometimes be rather too coarse for these. The sweeter or more lemon-flavoured types can be added to desserts.
Cosmetic Infuse leaves (with rosemary) as a hair rinse to deter dandruff. Use leaves in baths and facial steam baths.
Medicinal An infusion of the leaves can be very refreshing, as well as giving some relief from headaches and sore throats.
Household A strong decoction can be used as a household disinfectant. Use leaves in pot-pourri.

▼ *Thymus pulegioides* '**Bertram Anderson**' AGM   ▼ *Thymus* '**Doone Valley**'   ▼ *Thymus pulegioides* '**Foxley**'

Tussilago farfara

Coltsfoot

Description

THIS HARDY perennial reaches from 3–12in (7.5–30cm) in height, and has small, yellow flowers appearing in early spring. These are then followed by large, rounded, dark green, almost maple–like leaves, with grey undersides. Its small, white, spreading roots can make the plant invasive.

Recommended varieties

ONLY THIS species is available.

How to grow

USDA zone Z5
Site Full sun.
Soil Any moist soil.

Known uses

Ornamental appeal Not much! It is another of those plants that seem to excel on waste ground and ditches. Keep it to an uncultivated area of the herb garden.
Culinary Eat fresh leaves in salads. The flowers can be made into wine.
Cosmetic None.
Medicinal All parts of coltsfoot contain a mucilage, which is good for coughs and bronchitis. Decoct leaves for remedies for colds, flu and asthma.
Household None.

Propagation Sow seeds in spring; divide the crowns in autumn; or take root cuttings in spring or autumn.
Growing Lift and divide plants every two years to prevent them from becoming invasive. Growing coltsfoot in patio pots is a useful way to contain the plant. Keep well watered at all times.
Harvesting Pick and chop the leaves throughout summer, for using fresh or in preparation for drying. Harvest the flowers when available (early spring).

▼ *Tussilago farfara*

Ideas for using herbs

For a cook's garden

Alecost, angelica, basil, bay, bistort, borage, caraway, chervil, chives, coriander, dill, fennel, garlic, lemon balm, lovage, marjoram/ oregano, mint, parsley, rosemary, sage, savory, tarragon, thyme.

For edging, or front-of-border position

Box (clipped), catmint, chives, cotton lavender (clipped), feverfew, golden marjoram, hyssop (clipped), lavender (clipped), parsley, thyme, wall germander.

For the bath

Relaxing:
Catnip, chamomile, lavender.
Stimulating:
Basil, bay, fennel, lemon verbena, lovage, mint, rosemary, sage, thyme.
Healing:
Comfrey, chamomile, lady's mantle, mint, pot marigold, yarrow.

▼ **Lemon verbena**

For hedging

Box, cotton lavender, hyssop, lavender, *Rosa gallica officinalis*, rosemary, rue.

For walls and paving

Catmint, chamomile, feverfew, lavender (dwarf), pennyroyal, thyme, wall germander, winter savory.

For patio pots and troughs

Borage, catmint, coltsfoot, chamomile, chives, clary sage, lemon balm, mint (especially the round-leaved types), rosemary, sage, thyme.

For chalky soils

Chives, lavender, lemon balm, marjoram/oregano, rosemary, sage, salad burnet.

For moist or wet soils

Bergamot, bistort, comfrey, mints, sweet cicely.

▼ **Salad burnet**

For light or sandy soils

Alkanet, borage, bugle, chervil, chives, garlic, hyssop, lavender, lemon balm, lemon verbena, marjoram/oregano, rosemary, sage, savories, southernwood, tarragon, thyme, wormwood.

Annual herbs (to be replaced every year)

Anise, basil, borage, chervil, coriander, dill, florence fennel, marjoram (sweet), poppy (annual), purslane, summer savory.

Perennial herbs (continuing for three or more years)

Alecost, artemisia, bay, bergamot, bistort, chenopodium, chives, coltsfoot, cotton lavender, elder, fennel, lavender, lemon balm, liquorice, lovage, mint, rose, rosemary, rue, sage, sorrel, sweet cicely, tarragon, thyme, winter savory, yarrow.

Biennial herbs (requiring replacement every two years)

Alkanet, angelica, caraway, foxglove, mullein, parsley, woad.

For window boxes and hanging baskets

Basil, catmint, chives, clary, hyssop, lemon balm, marjoram/ oregano, nasturtium, parsley, pelargonium (especially the scented-leaved types), savory, tarragon.

▼ Hyssop

For adding to pot-pourris

Flowers:

Elder, lavender, rose, rosemary, thyme; as well as carnation and pink (*Dianthus* spp.), honeysuckle (*Lonicera* spp.), jasmine (*Jasminum* spp.) lily-of-the-valley (*Convallaria* spp.), mock orange (*Philadelphus* spp.), stock (*Matthiola* spp.), sweet pea (*Lathyrus* spp.), wallflower (*Erysimum* spp), lily (*Lilium* spp.) and hyacinth (*Hyacinthus* spp.).

Aromatic leaves:

Artemisia, bay, bergamot, coriander, lavender, pelargonium, rosemary, sage, thyme; as well as Mexican orange blossom (*Choisya* spp.), and sweet woodruff (*Asperula odorata*).

Seeds and spices:

Coriander, parsley; as well as Alexanders (*Smyrnium* spp.), allspice (*Pimenta* spp.), aniseed (*Pimpinella anisum*), cinnamon (*Cinnamomum* spp.), cloves (*Syzgium* spp.), nutmeg (*Myristica* spp.) and vanilla (*Vanilla* spp.).

To use in a garden for visually impaired people

Alecost, angelica, artemisia, basil, bergamot, chamomile, feverfew, hyssop, lavender, lemon balm, mint, pelargonium, rosemary, rue, sage, sweet cicely, tansy, thyme.

▼ *Lavandula* **'Regal Splendour'**

◀ *Pelargonium* **'Madame Salleron'**

Glossary

Acid soil
Soil that is deficient in lime and basic minerals; has a pH value below 7 (see pH scale, below).

Alkaline soil
Soil with a pH value above 7 (see pH scale, below).

Astringent
A substance that contracts living tissue. For example, an astringent cosmetic preparation tightens the skin.

Bolt/Bolting
Premature flowering and seed production, usually caused by plants being sown too early.

Bract
A modified or reduced leaf, generally set adjacent to the stalk of a flower or the flower itself.

Bulbil
A small bulb produced on the stem or in a leaf axil (or in the flower itself).

Bulblet
A small bulb produced from the existing bulb.

Compress
A piece of linen or cloth soaked in a herbal infusion or decoction and applied externally.

Cultivar
A cultivated plant clearly distinguished by one or more characteristics and which retains these characteristics when propagated; a contraction of 'cultivated variety', and often abbreviated to 'cv.' in plant naming.

Deadheading
The removal of spent flowers or flower heads.

Deciduous
Plant that loses its leaves at the end of every growing year, and which renews them at the start of the next.

Decoction
A herbal dose obtained by boiling a certain weight of herb in a certain quantity of liquid for a given length of time. Typically one uses 1oz (25g) of herb to 1pt (570ml) of water. A mild decoction is half this quantity of herb; a strong decoction is double the quantity of herb.

Diuretic
A substance that promotes the creation and/or flow of urine.

Double
Referred to in flower terms as a bloom with several layers of petals; usually there would be a minimum of 20 petals. 'Very double' flowers have more than 40 petals.

Evergreen
A plant that bears living foliage all year round.

Genus (pl. Genera)
A category in plant naming, comprising a group of related species.

Ground cover
Usually low–growing plants that grow over the soil, so suppressing weed growth.

Heel
The piece of bark or stem, which is retained on a shoot when it is taken for the purpose of propagation.

Hybrid
The offspring of genetically different parents, usually produced in cultivation, but occasionally arising in the wild.

Infusion
A herbal dose obtained by pouring a certain quantity of boiling liquid over a certain weight of herb, and leaving it to steep for a given length of time. Typically, 1oz (25g) of herb to 1pt (570ml) of water is used. A mild infusion is half this quantity of herb; a strong infusion is double the quantity of herb.

Macerate
To extract a drug from a plant (herb) by steeping it in a solvent.

Mucilage
A gelatinous substance, which occurs naturally in some herbs and is used to soothe and treat skin inflammation.

Mulch
Layer of material applied to the soil surface, to conserve moisture, improve its structure, protect roots from frost and suppress weeds.

Perennial
Plant that lives for at least three seasons.

pH scale
A scale measured from 1–14 that indicates the alkalinity or acidity of soil: pH 7 is neutral, pH 1–7 is acid and pH 7–14 is alkaline.

Poultice
Crushed herb (or plant) extracts, heated, squeezed (to reduce excess moisture) and then placed externally to soothe bruised or inflamed skin. Cover with a bandage or cotton strips to hold in place.

Rhizome/Rhizomatous
A stem formation at or below ground level; plants with this trait are rhizomatus.

Root-ball
The roots and surrounding soil or compost visible when a plant is removed from a pot.

Sideshoot
A stem that arises from the side of a main shoot or stem.

Single
In flower terms, a single layer of petals opening out into a fairly flat shape, comprising no more than five petals.

Species
A category in plant naming, the rank below genus, containing related, individual plants.

Stolon
A shoot that runs level with the soil, producing roots and shoots. Strawberry runners are a good example.

Sub-shrub
A plant that is woody at the base although the upper shoots die back in winter.

Sucker
Generally a shoot that arises from below ground, emanating from a plant's roots, but also refers to any shoot on a grafted plant that originates from below the graft union.

Tilth
A good, crumbly soil structure produced by careful cultivation and soil improvement. A fine tilth will be level and free of large lumps of soil and stones – ideal for sowing seeds.

Tincture
A solution of extracts of medicinal plants obtained by steeping them in alcohol (or an alcohol/water solution).

Topiary
Trees, shrubs and other ornamental plants that have been clipped into fanciful shapes and designs.

Tuber/Tuberous
A thickened, usually underground, storage organ derived from a stem or root; plants grown from tubers.

Umbel
A flat-topped mass of small flowers on stalks that radiate out from a central point, e.g. the *Achillea* flower head.

Variety
Botanically, a naturally occurring variant of a wild species; usually shorted to 'var.' in plant naming.

Useful websites

Garden Organic www.gardenorganic.org.uk
Growing herbs www.growingherbs.org.uk
Jekka's Herb Farm www.jekkasherbfarm.com
Mad About Herbs madaboutherbs.org
National Vegetable Society www.nvsuk.org.uk

Norfolk Herbs www.norfolkherbs.co.uk
Royal Horticultural Society www.rhs.org.uk
Suffolk Herbs www.suffolkherbs.com
The Herb Society www.herbsociety.org.uk

Further reading

A Modern Herbal by M. Grieve
(written 1931, published by Tiger Books, 1994)

Beginners' Guide to Herb Gardening by Yvonne Cuthbertson (published by Guild of Master Craftsman, 2001)

Complete Book of Herbs by Lesley Bremness
(published by Dorling Kindersley, 1988)

Cooking with Flowers by Jenny Leggatt
(published by Century Hutchinson, 1987)

Culpeper Complete Herbal
(published by Ware, 1995)

Encyclopedia of Herbs and Herbalism edited by Malcolm Stuart (published by Orbis, 1979)

Herbal by John Gerard
(written 1636; published by Bracken Books, 1985)

Natural Cures by Mark Evans
(published by Southwater, 1996)

RHS Encyclopedia of Herbs by Deni Bown
(published by Dorling Kindersley, 2008)

RHS Plant Finder
(published annually by Dorling Kindersley)

Scented Flora of the World by Roy Genders
(published by St Albans, 1978)

Success with Herbs by Yvonne Cuthbertson
(published by Guild of Master Craftsman, 2006)

The Ultimate Book of Herbs & Herb Gardening by Jessica Houdret (published by Lorenz, 1999)

About the author

Graham Clarke was born into gardening – literally. His father was in charge of the world-famous Regent's Park in London and at the time of Graham's birth the family lived in a lodge within the public gardens there. During his formative years Graham was surrounded by quality horticulture, so it was little surprise when he chose this as his career.

After he left school he studied with the Royal Horticultural Society at its Wisley Gardens in England, and it was here that he was for the first time exposed to the wonder of herbs and herbal culture. Today there is a large garden there devoted to decorative and functional herbs, but in Graham's day these plants were dotted all around the 150-acre garden, with only a small concentration of them within the Floral Department at Wisley.

After Wisley he worked as a gardener at Buckingham Palace in London, and his duties included tending the herbs there. This very private garden is seen by Her Majesty the Queen on most of the days she is in residence. For 30 years Graham has been a gardening writer and journalist. He has written 15 books, and countless articles for most of the major UK gardening magazines. At various times he was editor of *Amateur Gardening* (the UK's leading weekly magazine for amateurs) and *Horticulture Week* (the UK's leading weekly magazine for professionals), and he is now a freelance garden writer and consultant. He lives in Dorset, on England's south coast, with his wife and two daughters.

Picture credits

All of the pictures were taken by the author, except for those listed below:

GMC/Rebecca Mothersole: pages 2, 5, 6, 7 (both), 11, 13–16, 18 (bottom), 19 (bottom), 20 (bottom right), 21 (bottom), 22 (left top and bottom), 23 (left top), 24–29, 34 (bottom right), 35 (bottom right), 36 (bottom left), 39 (bottom right), 40 (bottom right), 41 (top right), 44, 46 (bottom), 48 (top), 54–58, 63 (bottom right), 65–66 (all), 68, 71, 74, 75 (bottom), 76, 78, 79 (bottom), 84, 86 (top right), 87 (both), 89, 91–93 (all), 96, 98 (first and second down), 99 (all), 100 (top and bottom), 101 (third down and bottom), 102.
GMC/Eric Sawford: 108–109 (all), 110 (bottom centre), 144, 147 (both).
Freda Cox: Illustration of an Ancient Egyptian Garden, p10.

Laurel Guilfoyle: 19 (top)
GMC/Anthony Bailey: 95
Flickr: 34 (top left).
Mr Fothergill's Seeds: 114, 120 (bottom right), 136 (bottom right), 157 (bottom right).
D.T. Brown Seeds: 140 (bottom left).

Herb illustrations by Michelle Willeter

GMC Publications would like to thank Wellingham Walled Herb Garden, Ringmer, Lewes, East Sussex for kindly allowing us to photograph their beautiful garden.

Index